Death of a Hero

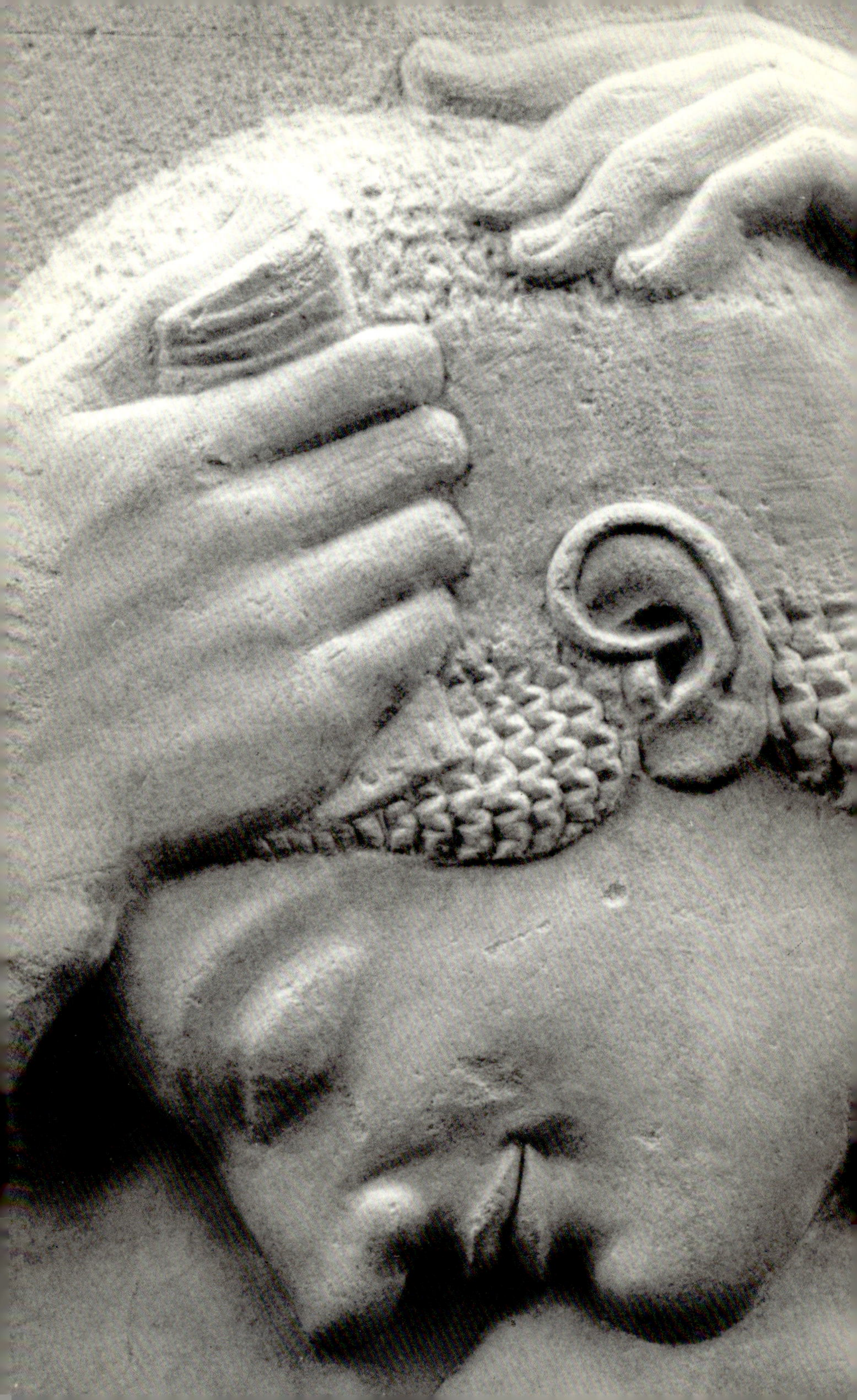

Death of a Hero

Jiří Frel

THE J. PAUL GETTY MUSEUM MALIBU, CALIFORNIA

17985 Pacific Coast Highway
Malibu, California 90265

ISBN number 0-89236-055-0 (hardcover)
0-89236-056-9 (paperbound)

Library of Congress catalogue number 84-804

Library of Congress Cataloging in Publication Data

Frel, Jiří.
Death of a hero.
Includes bibliographical references and index.
1. Sepulchral monuments—Greece. 2. Relief (Sculpture), Greek. 3. Death in art. 4. J. Paul Getty Museum. I. J. Paul Getty Museum. II. Title.
NB133.5.S46F7 1984 733′.3 84-804
ISBN 0-89236-055-0
ISBN 0-89236-056-9 (pbk.)

Table of Contents

D.M. Jean Deshayes

Eins in Drein sind Freunde:
Brüder von der Not,
Gleiche vor dem Feinde,
Freie vor dem Tod.
(F. Nietzsche)

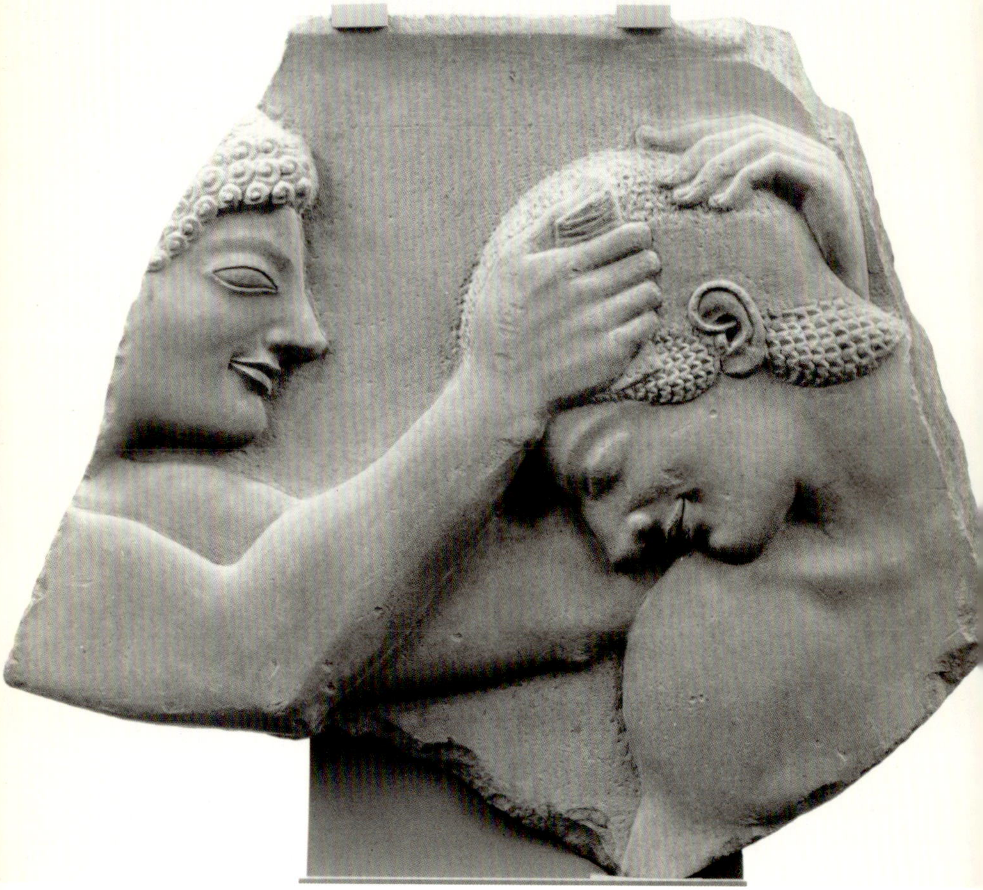

1. **Funerary monument of a young Athenian.** Ca. 520 B.C. Fine Parian marble, height: 49 cm, width: 59 cm. Malibu, The J. Paul Getty Museum 79.AA.1.

Two Friends

Two friends. Little remains from the monument but two heads and the upper torso and the arms of one reaching toward the other. With tenderness, the younger one winds a bandage around the wounded head of his companion. Nothing can separate the two friends, not even the death of one. Two and a half thousand years later the gravestone,[1] reduced to a miserable fragment, still preserves the magic of the art that confers apotheosis on the deceased youth and on the friendship of both forever.

Nothing is known about the two friends, for the night of time and the waters of Lethe have swallowed even their names. The style and workmanship of the sculpture provide the evidence that they were Athenians and that the tragic but heroic passing of the elder was commemorated by this monument between 520 and 510 B.C. The family must have been rich, for the stately monument was surely expensive, and its message expresses the ideas of the aristocracy, the cream of Athenian society of the time. The fragment is said to have been found in Anavysos,[2] southeast of Athens, in a very rich agricultural region. Other important funerary monuments found in this area might originally have stood in the same burial plot.[3]

These were the last years of the Athenian tyranny (neither tyrannic in the modern sense of the word nor lawless) of Hippias and Hipparchos, who had inherited the rule of Athens from their father Peisistratos. Although Peisistratos was twice expelled from Athens, he twice successfully returned and in time died peacefully as a respected and even beloved ruler in 527. At first nothing seemed to change after his death. The sons continued the father's policies. Under their administration, the cultural blossoming of the city peaked dramatically, in part a result of the economic expansion during the previous years. The new, large temple of the city's patron goddess Athena on the Acropolis was completed in marble with extensive sculptural decoration, and a crowd of votive offerings filled the Acropolis. The Persian king's penetration into Asia Minor, not generally favorable for the politics of the Peisistratids, brought to Athens a stream of artists looking for work and a safe haven. Famous musicians and poets (at this time often one and the same man) like Anakreon and Simonides came, as did sculptors and painters. Unfortunately the Peisistratids did not succeed in overcoming Athens' internal contradictions, which were aggravated by the

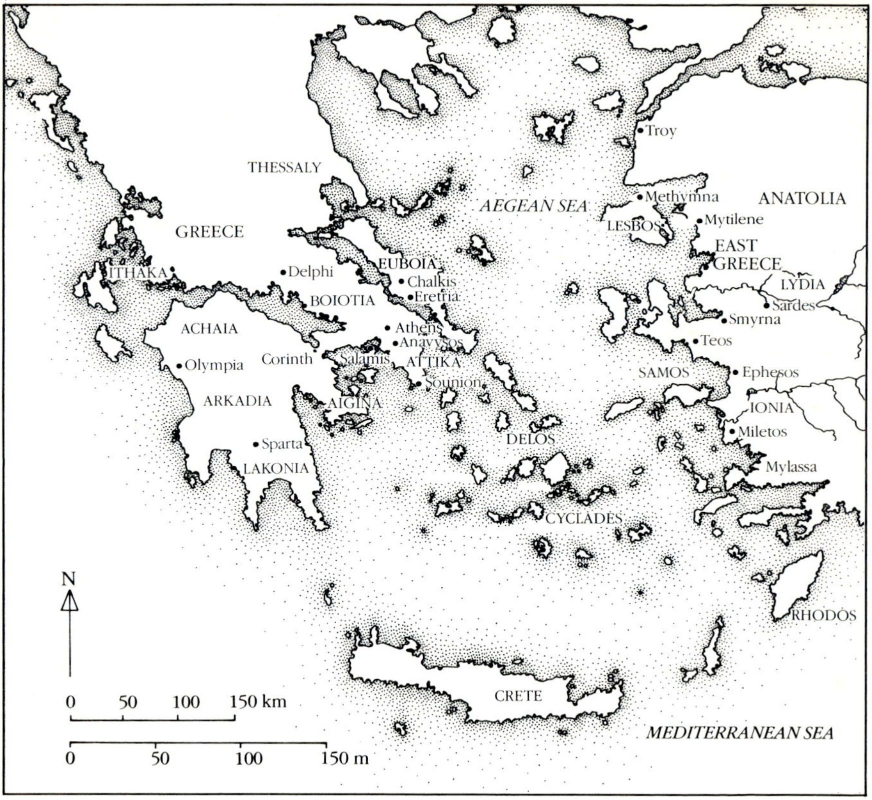

2. **Map of Greece**. Drawing by Martha Breen Bredemeyer.

general situation throughout all Greece as the Persian menace polarized the Greek city states as much as did the forces inside them.

In 514 Hipparchos was killed by two aristocrats, the young Harmodios and the older Aristogeiton, close friends. A decade later, the victorious democracy made them Athenian national heroes (fig. 3), even though their conspiracy had had only private motives and failed. However, dislike of the tyranny was widespread. Not only the old-fashioned aristocrats (landowners and gentleman farmers) but also the craftsmen and merchants, fishermen and sailors, and the deprived poor were united at least in the struggle against tyranny. In the year 510 this democratic front, led by the Alkmaionids, an exiled aristocratic clan, finally succeeded in exiling the tyrant Hippias into the arms

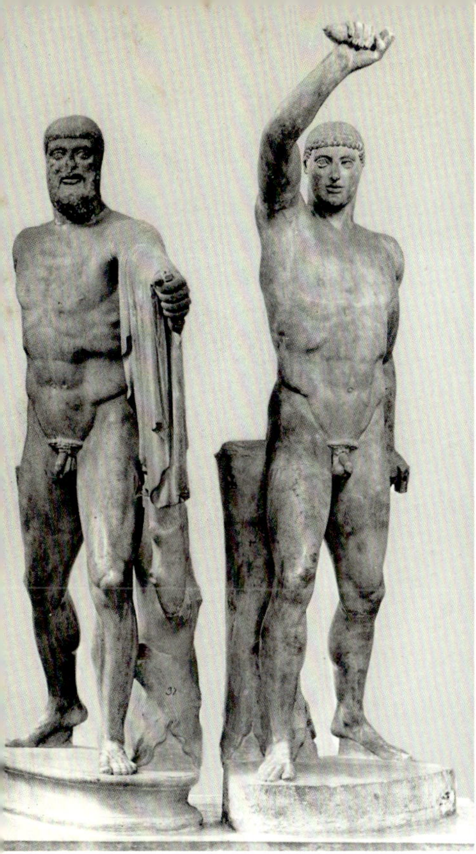

3a. **Tyrant Slayers.** Roman marble copies after the original group by Kritias and Nesiotes, erected in 476/5 B.C. in the Athenian marketplace. Naples, National Museum.

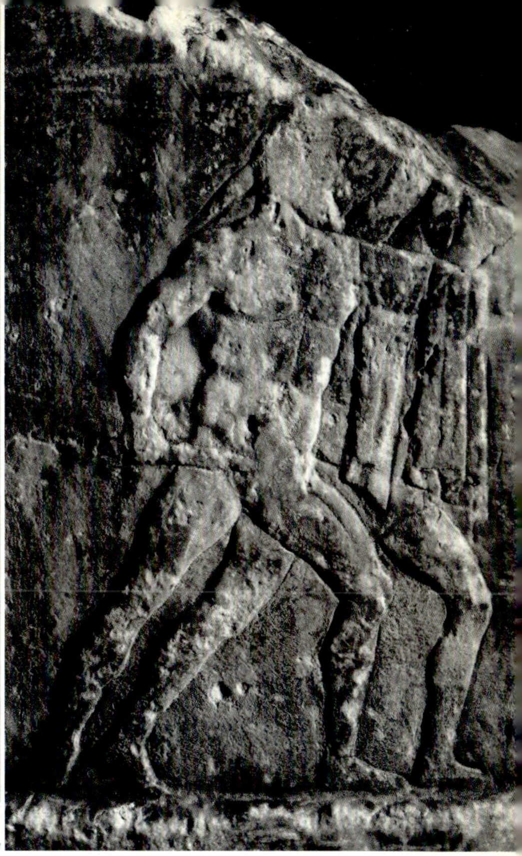

3b. **Tyrant Slayers.** Detail of relief representation of the group by Kritias and Nesiotes on the right side of the Elgin Throne, from Athens. Malibu, The J. Paul Getty Museum.

of the Persian king with the help of Sparta, pushed by the bribed Delphic oracle.

War was frequent in these agitated times, and a wellborn Athenian had plenty of opportunities to fulfill his first patriotic duty. It was in some military event after 520 that the older of these two friends met his destiny. Following the funeral or slightly later, the relief was erected over his grave (possibly as a cenotaph, if the body was not recovered) in the family funerary plot.

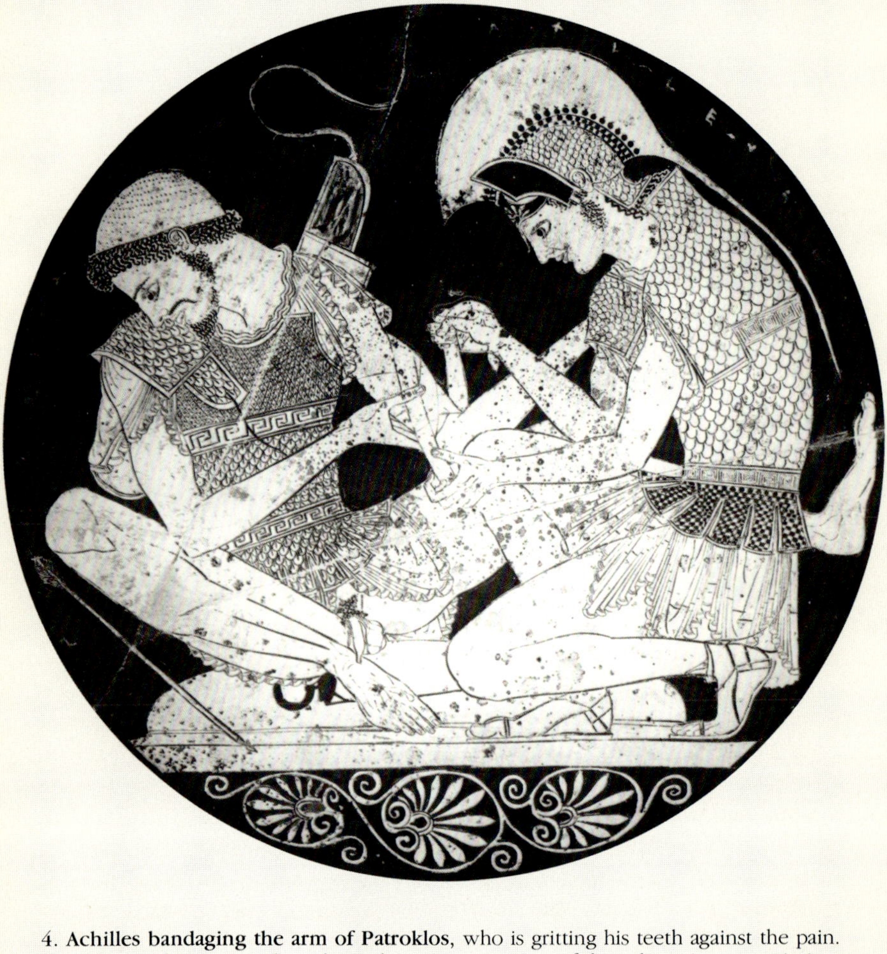

4. **Achilles bandaging the arm of Patroklos,** who is gritting his teeth against the pain. Ca. 510 B.C., this cup tondo is the earliest representation of the subject in vase painting. Berlin, Staatliche Museen.

What is Represented

Nothing is known about the man who carved the relief. Did he ever personally know the two friends? How did he feel about the blow that struck one to a tragic glory? In any case his personal views were unimportant. He was not supposed to capture the actual appearance of the two youths nor to describe the exact circumstances of the demise. Following the canons of his craft, he commemorated the family's grief and pride in its son and his friend.

The word the Greeks used for a funerary monument was *sema*—sign, marker. Few of the gravestones of the sixth century survive, and there were probably not too many erected. The quality is mostly outstanding: it seems that only an exceptional death of an exceptional man deserved a memorial. A standard archaic grave relief depicts the noble deceased. The representation of two persons is rare, and the depiction of action is extremely unusual. Such is, however, the subject of the Getty monument. The younger one is supporting the wounded head of his dying friend with one hand, while winding a bandage around it with the other. This representation of binding a wound is the first instance of a very rare subject in Greek art. In the tondo of a red-figure cup made slightly later, about 510 B.C., Achilles bandages the wounded arm of his friend Patroklos, who is baring his teeth in a grimace of pain (fig. 4).[4] Still later, about 480 B.C., a wounded man is shown being bandaged on a red-figure aryballos (fig. 5), the name piece of the so-called Clinic Painter.[5]

The gesture of caressing the back of the head to express support and affection is more common. It appears on a slightly earlier grave relief by the same artist where a seated mother cradles the head of her dead child (fig. 6, see p. 49),[6] but the more frequent meaning of the gesture was to express erotic affection. Thus in a *symposion* on a Greek wall painting from the first quarter of the fifth century from Paestum,[7] a bearded man caresses the nape of a young companion who tries to push him gently away (fig. 7). In some other cases the connotation is even more clearly erotic, as on a red-figure cup by the Triptolemos Painter from about 480 B.C. that shows a couple, where the woman caresses the head of her companion with evident affection (fig. 8).[8] Finally a similar gesture, but with both hands engaged, commonly marked the consolation provided to a man who drank more than was good for him.[9] The affection on the Getty relief is, of course, of

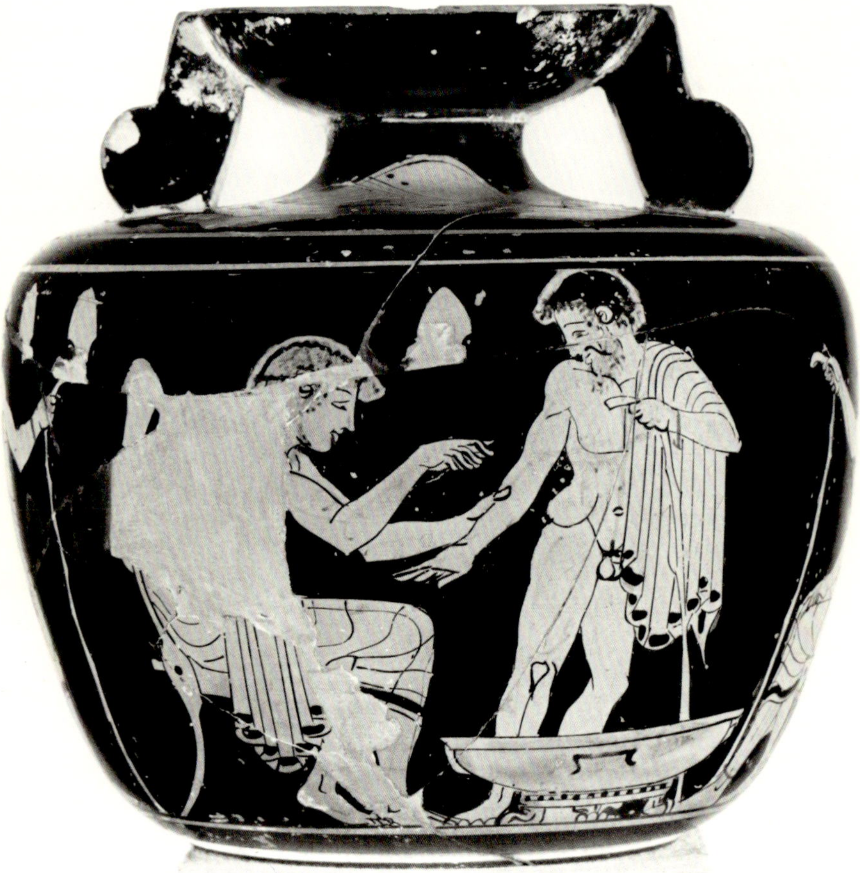

5. Examining the arm of a wounded man. The intent professionalism of the physician and the trepidation of the patient are well conveyed. The name piece of the Clinic Painter, ca. 480 B.C. Paris, Louvre.

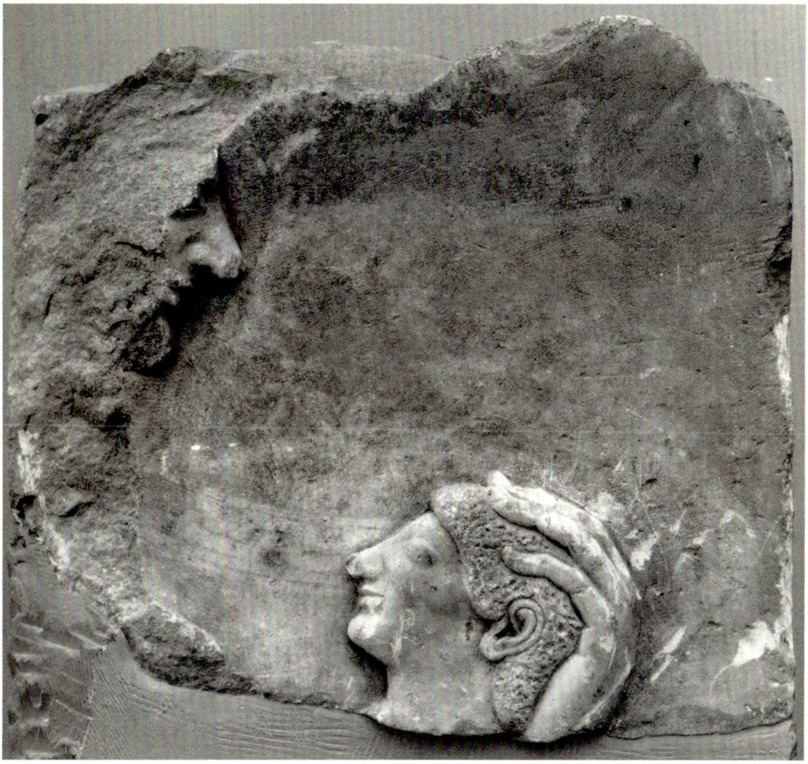

6. Woman cradling the head of her dead child. Fragment of a grave stele, probably a funerary monument for both of them, by the same hand as the Getty relief. Erected at Anavysos ca. 530 B.C. Note the traces of paint for the woman's mantle between her shoulder and the child's head. Athens, National Museum.

another kind; but the gesture remains the same.

The profiles of the youths correspond to their different ages. The younger man's head is less well preserved; but his face still shows the soft contours of boyhood, and he is less tall. The larger profile of the older youth's face is placed lower in the panel. He is bent forward, collapsing in agony. His closed eye expresses the imminence of death, just as death is indicated by the lidded eye of the little child on the grave relief mentioned above (figs. 6, 51),[10] that of the hero Sarpedon drawn by Euphronios, the great master of Attic vase painting some years before 510 B.C. (fig. 11),[11] and that of the dead Achilles painted by the Berlin Painter just after 500 B.C. (fig. 12).[12] Even Zeus, the supreme

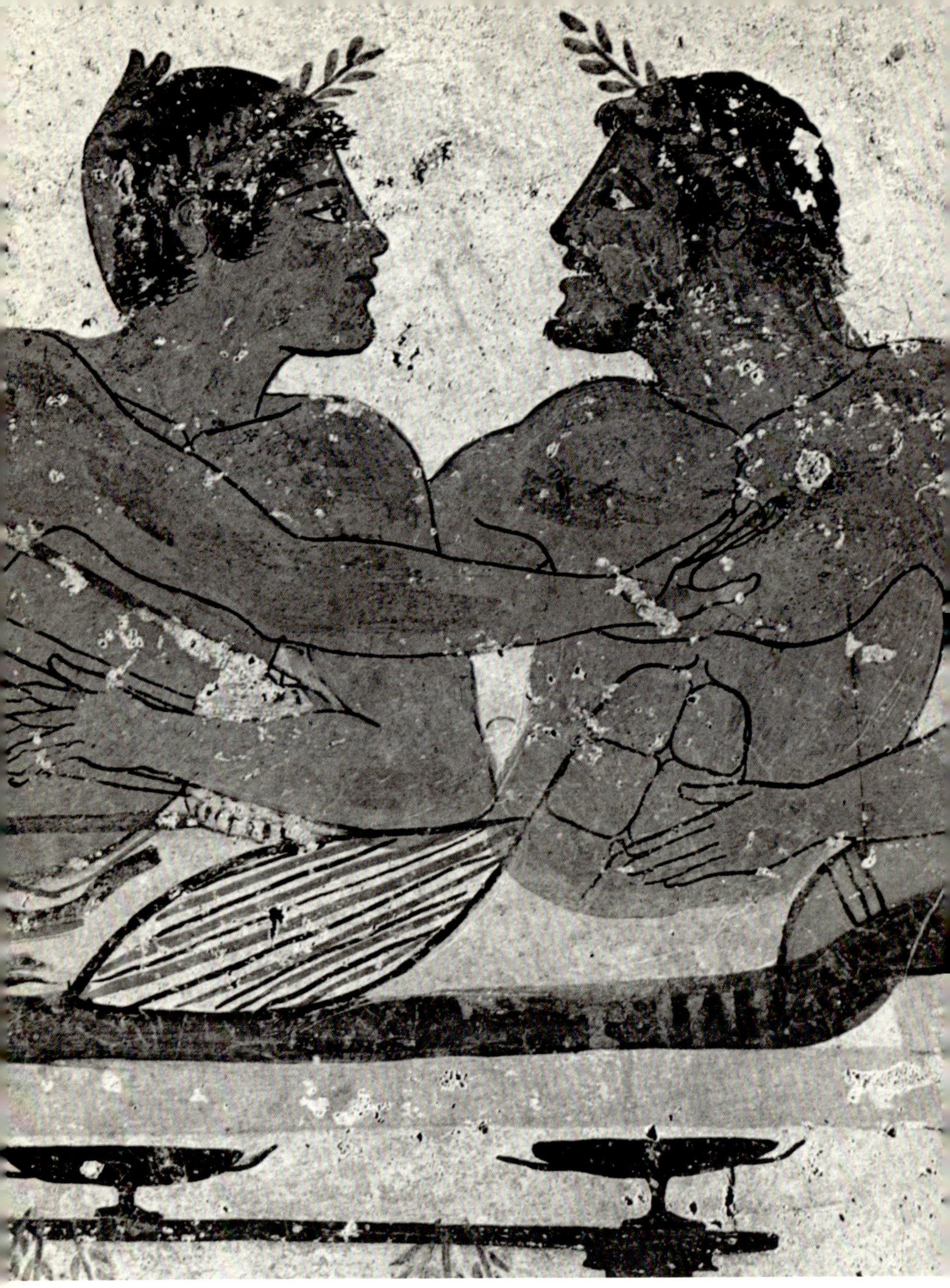

7. **Eromenos and erastes at a symposion**. The affectionate gesture of stroking the head is gently rebuffed by the young musician. Greek wall painting in a tomb at Paestum (Poseidonia), south of Naples. After 480 B.C.

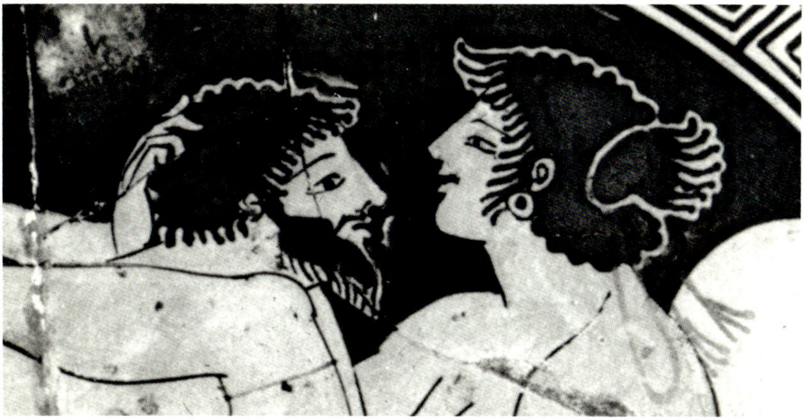

8. Lovers. The woman caresses the head of her companion. Red-figure cup ca. 480 B.C. by the Triptolemos Painter. Tarquinia, Museo Nazionale.

king of both gods and mortals, could not save his own son Sarpedon from his inevitable destiny in the man-devouring battle before the holy city of Troy. But Zeus at least secured Sarpedon's glory and preserved his body for an appropriate funeral. Nor can the dying youth on the Getty relief be brought back to life, not even by the painstaking efforts of his young friend, who not only binds his wounded head but also provides the most tender support to prevent his total collapse.

And yet, there is more. To the modern eye the smiling expression of the younger companion's face may appear indifferent, but to his contemporaries it mirrored the intense although vain attempt to hold his dying friend on this side of the great barrier. In archaic art, no despair is allowed: the youth keeps smiling. The same delicate smile animates the faces of most figures in Greek art of the sixth century B.C., a smile that provides men and women, mortal or immortal, with the divine spark of life and a suitable appearance in any situation, even the most difficult, even despair and death. The smile of the older youth stems from the same tradition, but its meaning is different. He has already transcended the bonds of mortal flesh and, while still physically present, he is approaching freedom from pain and blood, joining the gods as a *heros athanatos,* an immortal hero. Indeed, this smile transforms his journey into an apotheosis, marking his death as a *kalos thanatos,* the beautiful death of a young hero.[13]

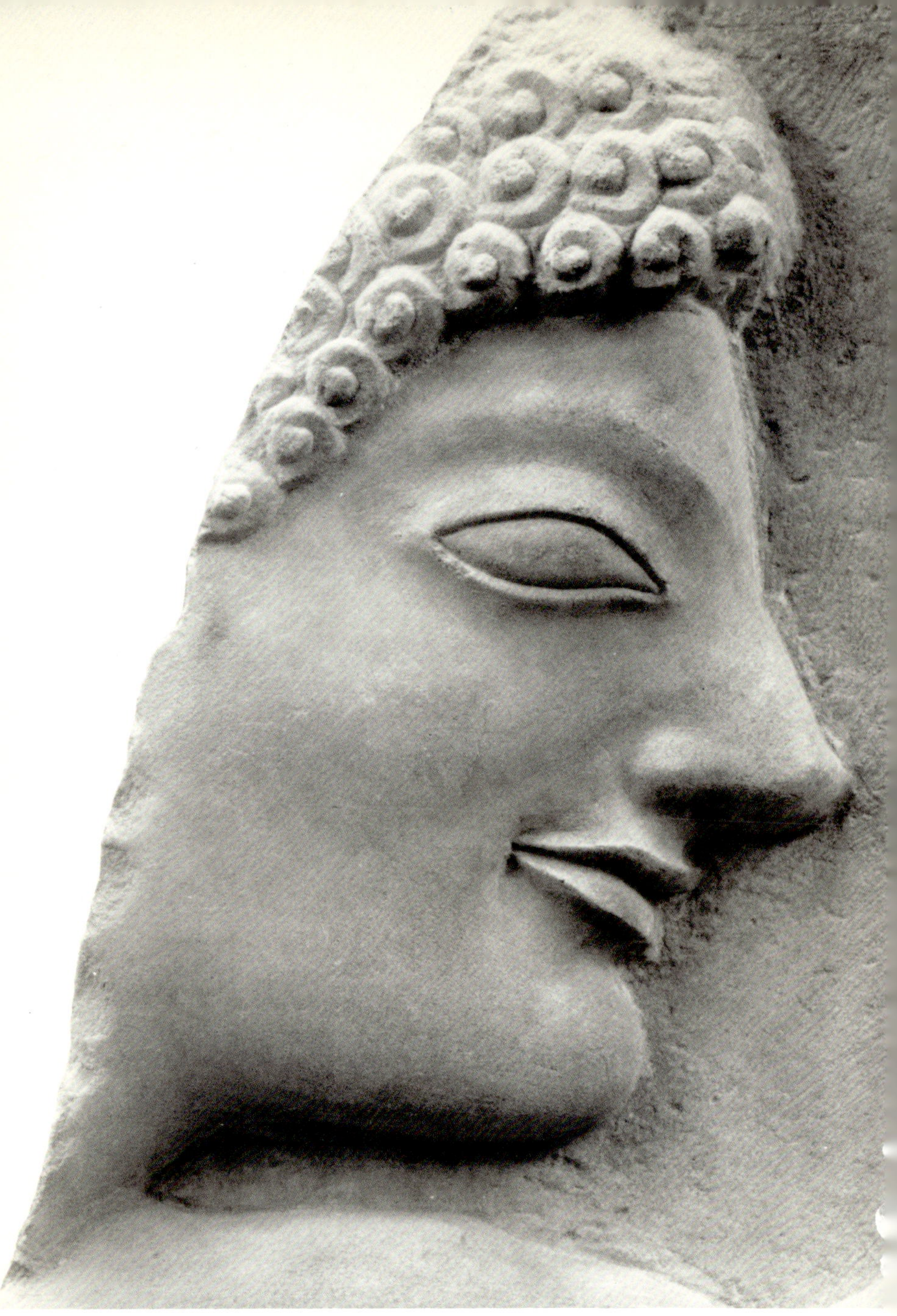

9. **Head of the younger man** on the Getty relief.

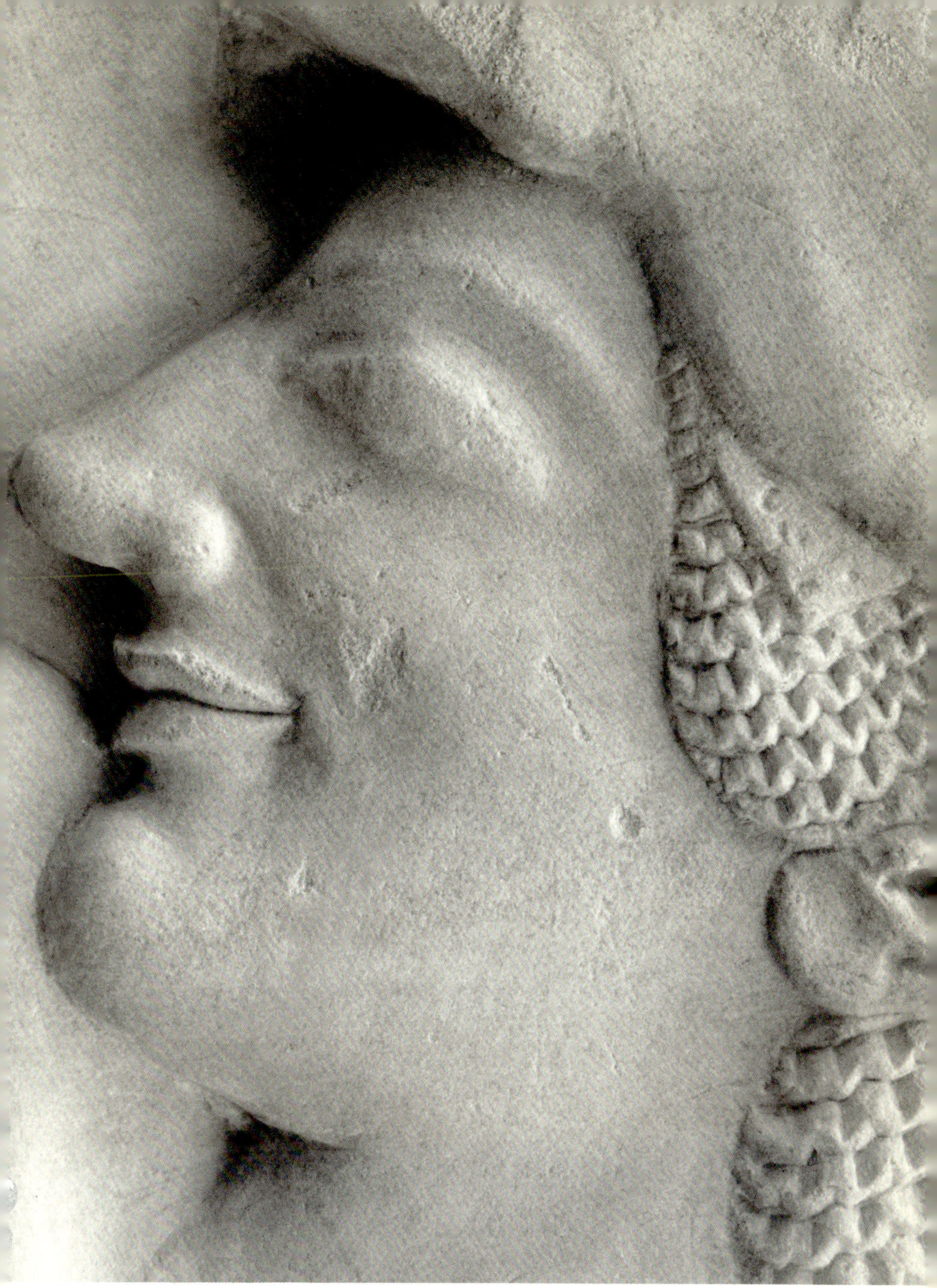

10. Head of the dying man on the Getty relief. The closed eyes and the looser modeling show him relaxing into death.

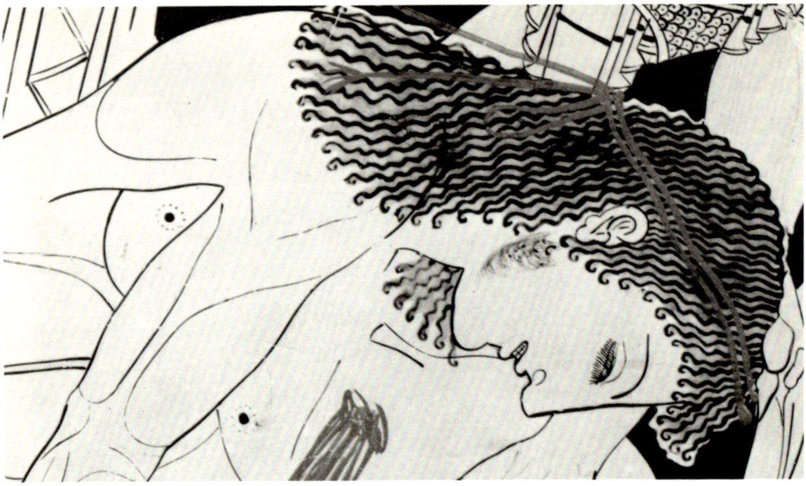

11. **Head of the dead Sarpedon** from a red-figure calyx krater signed by Euphronios (detail of fig. 13). Before 510 B.C. The closed eyes indicate death. New York, The Metropolitan Museum of Art.

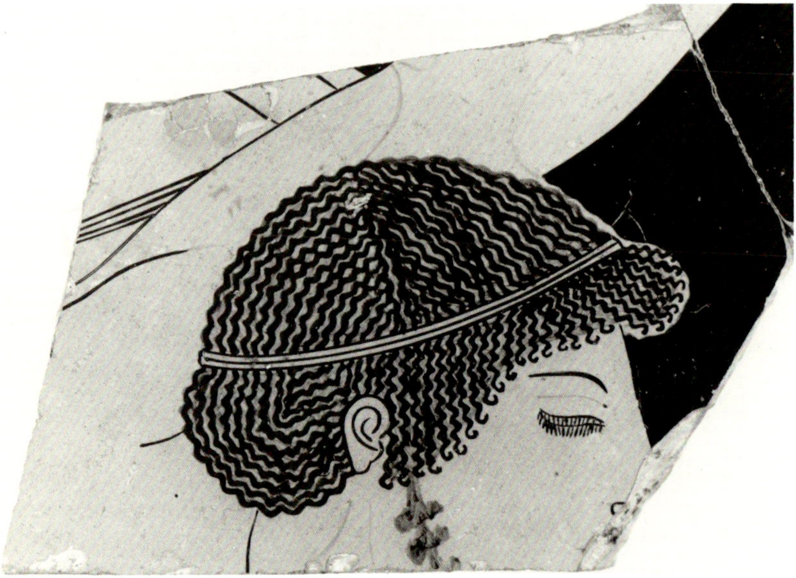

12. **Head of the dead Achilles**, with closed eyes. Fragment of a red-figure calyx krater attributed to the Berlin Painter. Just after 500 B.C. Malibu, The J. Paul Getty Museum.

Kalos Thanatos

The youth who dies on the battlefield is considered fortunate and beautiful, for he rises above the human condition, closer to the gods, by confronting the inevitable with courage and determination. In all ancient Greek art, *kalos thanatos* provides an appropriate opportunity to exalt the heroic ideal. Its origins go far back. The idea was formulated for all time in the Homeric poems, where it runs as a continuous undercurrent within the tissue of the narrative, reaching its most poignant expression in Priam's words exhorting Hektor. The father and king insists on the contrast between the ugliness and horror of the bloody, decrepit body of a slain old warrior and the beautiful appearance of a dead young hero. Priam's actual intention is far from inciting Hektor to a premature death, however glorious: the old king is revealed as a poor father desperately trying to save the only protection of holy Troy and of his own old age by persuading his son to retire behind the city walls and not perish in a hopeless fight against Achilles. Hektor can only refuse.[14]

> But if so many of my [sons] are dead already and gone down to the
>   house of Hades,
> it is sorrow to our hearts, who bore them, myself and their mother,
> but to the rest of the people a sorrow that will be fleeting
> beside their sorrow for you, if you go down before Achilles.
> Come then inside the wall, my child, so that you can rescue
> the Trojans and the women of Troy, neither win the high glory
> for Peleus' son, and yourself be robbed of your very life. Oh, take
> pity on me, the unfortunate still alive, still sentient
> but ill-starred, whom the father, Kronos' son, on the threshold of
>   old age
> will blast with hard fate, after I have looked upon evils
> and seen my sons destroyed and my daughters dragged away captive
> and the chambers of marriage wrecked and the innocent children taken
> and dashed to the ground in the hatefulness of war, and the wives
> of my sons dragged off by the accursed hands of the Achaians.
> And myself last of all, my dogs in front of my doorway
> will rip me raw, after some man with a stroke of the sharp bronze
> spear, or with a spearcast, has torn the life out of my body;
> those dogs I raised in my halls to be at my table, to guard my
> gates, will lap my blood in the savagery of their anger

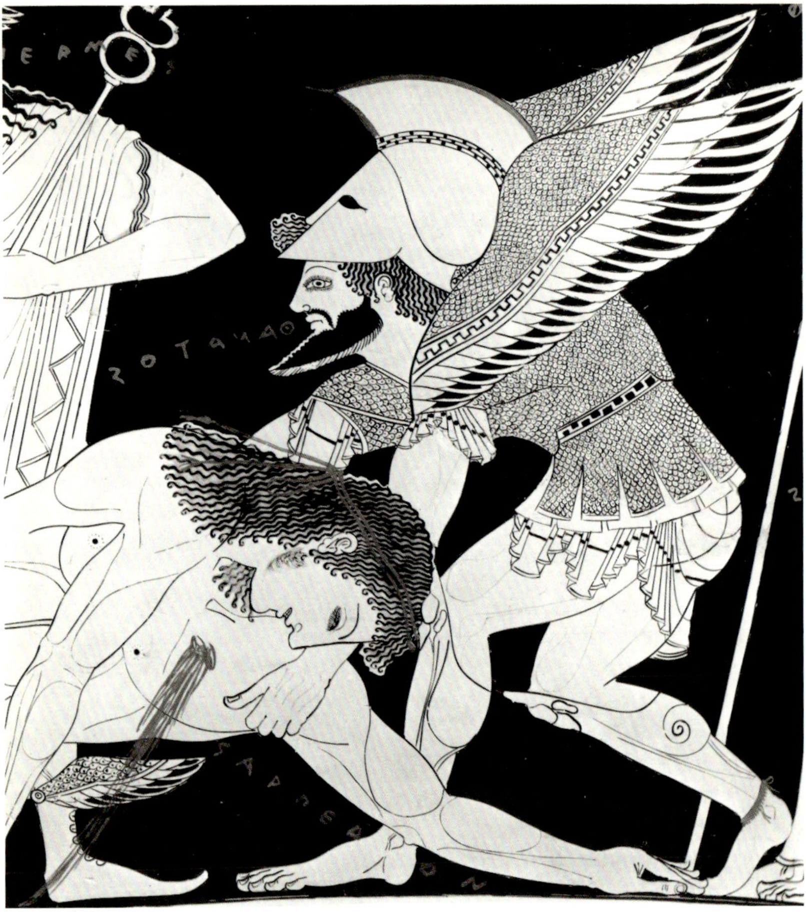

13. **The dead Sarpedon carried by Death and Sleep**, guided by Hermes (see also fig. 11). This episode from the myth of the hero Sarpedon, the son of Zeus who died before Troy, illustrates the respectful glory that surrounded death in battle.

and then lie down in my courts. For a young man all is decorous
when he is cut down in battle and torn with the sharp bronze,
    and lies there
dead, and though dead still all that shows about him is beautiful;
but when an old man is dead and down, and the dogs mutilate
the gray head and the gray beard and the parts that are secret,
this, for all sad mortality, is the sight most pitiful.

With cruel logic, Priam's unheeded exhortation reaches a heartbreaking coda. Priam, guided and protected by the immortal gods, has to enter the Greek camp, where he humbly kisses the hands of Achilles, those that had slain countless of his sons, in order to ransom Hektor's body. The gods, for whom the pious Hektor always had a pleasant sacrifice, could not prevent his slaughter however much they loved him. But after his death at least two gods, Aphrodite and Apollo, were continuously engaged in protecting his body, preventing its decay, and maintaining its youthful splendor. The case is not unique: Zeus himself instructed Apollo to supervise the transport of the body of Sarpedon, Zeus' own son, and to keep it intact and beautiful for the funeral (fig. 13). In a similar way, Thetis, Achilles' mother, infused nectar and ambrosia into the nostrils of the dead Patroklos, her son's best friend, in order to preserve his radiant beauty.

The gods, as expert morticians, disguise the tragic destiny of men. What a superb fig leaf covers the empty illusion, devised in order to protect the status of leaders blessed by the gods and to hide from man's own eyes the unspeakable misery of the human condition. But also what an exalting, heart-touching idea is *kalos thanatos,* when compared with the illusion of another epoch, built up on exactly the same pattern and pushed to a diabolic mockery by the pious man Dostoevsky: the heart of Alyosha, the nicest of the Karamazovs, breaks when his beloved *starets* Zosima fails to die according to the standards established for true holy people. Instead of producing the expected celestial odor from his dead flesh, Zosima stank, as will the decaying corpses of us all.

For a Homeric hero, *kalos thanatos* is something like a natural law. In all the Homeric poems, there is just one attempt to state that life is preferable to the heroic reputation: Thersites, an ugly, foul-tongued coward, is instantly and painfully silenced with the joyful approval of the common people. However, already before the end of the seventh century, a strong voice was raised against this venerable ideal. The great lyrical poet Archilochos, the first tangible exponent of the individual in Greek literature, blandly admits in a poem that he did not hesitate to throw away his shield as he ran for his life in a lost battle, an epitome of inadmissible cowardice for a wellborn man, a *kalos kai agathos,* through all archaic and classical Greece.

In the merciless glare of the passage of time, the heroic false consciousness of Homeric Greece may not make sense; but Homeric ideas constituted the stem of the flower that was Greece. *Kalos thana-*

tos, death on the battlefield, later found perhaps its most concise apotheosis in Perikles' funeral allocution immortalizing democracy. In a similar speech, he stated: "We do not see the gods, but we know they exist from the sacrifices we offer them and from the welfare they provide the city. The same is true about the heroes who fell for the native land."[15] The great Athenian statesman must have been personally aware to some extent of the falseness of the consciousness, since he added with some unmistakable melancholy a further comment about the fallen youth: "The year has lost its spring."

None of this sad awareness of the later fifth century is expressed in the Getty relief. It belongs to a still younger world, when the umbilical cord between man and society was a strong and natural necessity. The sacrifice of a young life did not yet require a rhetorical justification. The historian Herodotos later expressed these traditional feelings when describing how in the first half of the sixth century Solon, the retired elder statesman who was still an active businessman and didactic poet (elevated by later generations to the status of one of the legendary Seven Wise Men), visited Kroisos, the proverbially rich king of Lydia in Asia Minor, at his capital of Sardis.[16] It took a long time for the king's servants to show Solon all of the royal treasures before Kroisos received his visitor in a private audience.

> "Well, Athenian guest, whom do you think to be the luckiest man in the world?"
>
> "Telos the Athenian, King."
>
> Kroisos was disappointed, as he always flattered himself on his good fortune: "Telos who?"
>
> "Indeed, Mr. Nobody. An Athenian like any other."
>
> "All right, my wise man. But how do you reckon his claim to be the luckiest?"
>
> "He was born a free citizen while the majority of humans were subjects of monarchs, if not slaves, and his city was prosperous in his lifetime. Male children were born to him and remained alive, growing into good citizens. And he even saw the children born to his sons: male were they, and they remained alive. And he fell in battle when the victory was already sure."

Men Among Men

The dying youth on the Getty relief must have fallen on the battlefield to his parents' pride and grief. Still in the spring of his life, he might not have begotten any children, but at least he had a friend who stood close to him in combat. He may even have taken the blow that was aimed at the other. Close in death and close in life, the two were more than friends. To understand such a relationship no analogy can be drawn with any other time, especially our own. Ancient Greece was a world of men, an exclusive society of men for men. Even at the democracy's apogee in the fifth century B.C., Athens, the same city that welcomed alien permanent residents and was indulgent toward her slaves, did her best to ignore her female citizens. In his famous funeral oration lauding democracy, Perikles uttered but one condescending sentence toward women: "The only thing they should legitimately aspire to, is not to be spoken about either for bad or for good."[17] Remaining inconspicuous, women citizens had the privilege of giving birth to free citizens. But children belonged completely to the father. As Aristotle "scientifically" explains it, the initiation of life is in the semen, while the pregnant woman provides only the place for the child to grow and the nutrition. If free women were poor, they were also allowed to do hard work in the fields. They participated in some sacrifices, but they were banished from the political life of their community. Banished is the wrong word—it simply did not exist for them. As women they were excluded from the essential cultural activities of the city, especially from any involvement in the *gymnasion,* the real center of Greek life. Women also did not participate in many public festivities or in the daily joys of life such as *symposia* unless they were less than respectable.

Throughout ancient Greece, men remained alone among themselves, although only in Sparta were they actually confined to barracks for all their adult life. In Sparta also two male friends were placed next to each other in the battle line, their mutual friendship urging on their courage. In Athens life was more gentle, but even there the two friends of the Getty relief were probably placed side by side in the battlefront. A funerary monument dating about 500 B.C. represents such a situation: two warriors aligned in close association, perhaps in an ambush (fig. 29).[18] The friends would have gone together through military training, the elder helping with the instruction of the younger.

They surely exercised together daily in the *gymnasion,* which was the natural social center of the city, preparing for service under arms. They participated side by side in other games and festivities, the older always protecting and helping the younger. Occasionally, he would show his affection with love gifts like pet animals, a hare or a cock. Cocks were trained for fighting (even Zeus appears in vase painting offering his beloved Ganymede a cock), but the hare was considered an especially appropriate love present.

The usual words describing such friends were *erastes* (lover) for the older one and *eromenos* (the beloved one) for the younger. This type of male relationship, an ephebic beauty protected by someone of experience, found countless reflections in contemporary art, especially in vase painting. Beautiful *ephebes*—teenagers—are standard figures in scenes of athletics, musical performances, banquets, and courting. The names of particularly handsome and famous beauties were written on vases with the adjective *kalos* (beautiful) appended, often with no relationship to the scene depicted.[19] These handsome youths were most often the offspring of the best Athenian families. One of the most celebrated of them, Leagros,[20] later fell on the battlefield as a general.[21] His son Glaukos followed his father's example, both as a *kalos*-acclaimed youth on vases[22] and as a military officer.[23] The seventy-odd surviving acclamations of Leagros fall into the fifteen years between 515 and 500 B.C., but this long duration is rather an exception, and Leagros must have been an unusual case. Most acclamations appear on vases for a period of less than ten years. The flowerlike beauty of a developing youth is ephemeral, and his fame does not last.

Such must have been the relationship of our two friends, the older caring for the younger, protecting him and introducing him into the world of men. Probably the final instance of their friendship occurred on the battlefield, where the *erastes* might have taken the blow aimed at his *eromenos.* Contemporaries would have understood this event as the one preceding the scene of the relief where their standard roles are suddenly reversed: with all his soul the younger one succors his friend.

The idea of such a friendship goes back to Homer. Indeed, it is the core of the friendship of Achilles and Patroklos. Patroklos momentarily oversteps the boundary line when he believes his friend Achilles wrong and borrows his armor to represent him in battle. Patroklos thus commits an act of hubris which brings his inevitable death. Burning to take revenge, Achilles rejects the warning of his mother Thetis not to kill Hektor as his destiny was to die soon after: "Right now I should be dead as I did not help my friend in need."[24] The "friend in need" resounds throughout all of Greek tradition. Achilles and Patroklos' friendship was remembered by Alexander the Great, who was imbued with Homer, and by his closest friend Hephaistion. Destiny allowed Alexander to mourn his friend in a truly Homeric manner, and in Homeric style Alexander did not survive Hephaistion long afterwards.

At the time of the Getty relief, the most famous example of such a friendship was provided by a pair of aristocrats, young Harmodios and the already-bearded Aristogeiton, who perished in a vain attempt to take personal revenge on the Athenian tyrants Hippias and Hipparchos. Succeeding in killing only Hipparchos, they were slain immediately afterwards; but by an irony of history they soon became heroes for the new Athenian democracy, champions of liberty, and a patriotic cliché for centuries of school-age children. The statues of the *Tyrannicides* (Tyrant Slayers)[25] were erected in the Agora (fig. 3), the Athenian marketplace, engraved with a short poem which commemorated their deed by an apt and probably intentional misinterpretation:

> A great light showed upon Athenians when Aristogeiton and Harmodios slew Hipparchos
> [--------missing one verse-------------------------
> ----and half a verse----] established their native land.[26]

Statues of the *Tyrannicides* were, in fact, erected twice. The first group, cast by the Athenian sculptor Antenor, was looted by the Persian king Xerxes from occupied Athens in 480. It was restored to Athens more than a hundred and fifty years later by Alexander the Great. We have no direct information about this monument, but it was not substantially different from the second bronze version which the Athenians commissioned just after restoring their burned city in 477/6 from Kritios and Nesiotes, followers of Antenor in the same studio. Both images from the later version survive in Roman copies and in reproductions on works of Greek minor arts; an example is the small scale relief on the so-called Elgin throne in the J. Paul Getty Museum.[27]

The story of the Tyrant Slayers provides a warning against projecting modern ideas into antiquity. Aristogeiton's friendship for Harmodios did not prevent him from having a girl friend. Her (probably adopted) name was Leaina, the "lioness," suitable for a pleasure girl. Whatever her social status may have been, she participated in the conspiracy of the Tyrant Slayers and later also in their glory. She was of strong character. When investigated under torture, she bit off her tongue so as not to reveal any secrets; and she perished, becoming a martyr of freedom. Aristogeiton's friendship with Harmodios followed the established, if not obligatory, social pattern, while nature brought him into the arms of Leaina. Something similar may have happened to Leagros when he was growing out of the ephebic years. On a red-figure cup from the very beginning of the fifth century,[28] a pleasure girl of barbarian origin (indicated by the intentional scarification covering her naked body) lies in the arms of a youth who has just started to grow a peach-fuzz beard; his name is inscribed in the medallion: Leagros.

The Fashion of Hair

The formal statement of the Getty relief is expressed with a minimum of props. The only attribute is the bandage, suggesting that the scene follows a battle. This was clue enough for the Athenians at the end of the sixth century, and it should be sufficient also for today's viewer. The same simplicity also governs the presentation of both human figures, with one exception. The artist emphasizes the splendid hair styles with a great indulgence of detail. Each youth sports a different style. The strands of the younger one's hair style terminate in snail-shaped curls above his forehead (fig. 14), while the elder's hair is a crown of tightly crimped waves (fig. 16). Both fashions appear simultaneously on another monument of the same period by the same artist, the central group of the west pediment of the temple of Apollo Daphnephoros in Eretria, representing Theseus abducting Antiope, the queen of Amazons (fig. 15).[29] Theseus' hair is fashioned like the rounded curls of the younger man on the Getty relief, while the spiky strands of Antiope (fig. 17) correspond to the hair of the dying youth. Originally the elaborate hair styles were further enhanced by the rich polychromy of the whole relief, and the hair of each was probably gilded. Gilding rarely survives on ancient sculpture after it has been uncovered, but some examples are known. For a few months in 1959 visitors to the Kerameikos Museum could admire the traces of gilding, until it faded before their eyes, in the hair of Eupheros[30] on his fine later fifth-century grave stele (fig. 18). The tradition of gilded hair continued into Roman times; the muses carved around A.D. 200 for the niches on the facade of the theater in Kremna (in southwest Asia Minor), some of which are in the Getty Museum,[31] still show perceptible traces of gold in their hair (fig. 19).

This exuberance of hair design, further enhanced by color and gilding, may seem today an over-rich decorative effect, but the original intention was not just ornamental. Both Sarpedon and Achilles in vase paintings of the period (figs. 11 and 12 above) are distinguished by extremely elaborate hairstyles that must have added to their dignity. As so often, the tradition goes back to Homer. Describing the irresistible beauty of Hektor's brother Euphorbos, who was slain by Patroklos, the poet states "his hair was like the hair of the Graces, and his tresses were braided with gold and silver."[32] Vase painting also clarifies what fine hairdressing meant to the Greeks. On the best-known calyx krater

14. Head of the younger man on the Getty relief. The strong side light enhances the sharply delicate modeling of the youth's profile and features.

15 a and b. Head of Theseus from the west pediment of the temple of Apollo Daphnephoros (see fig. 56). The profile reveals a three-dimensional relative of fig. 14, including the same snail-curl hair style; the greater delicacy is due both to the roundness and to the sculptor's greater maturity. Chalkis, Museum.

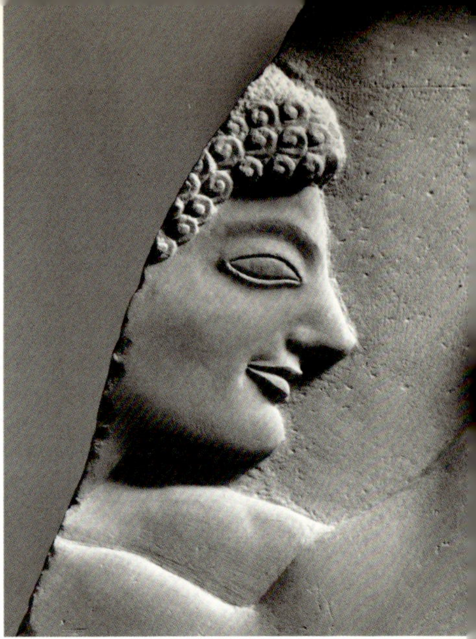

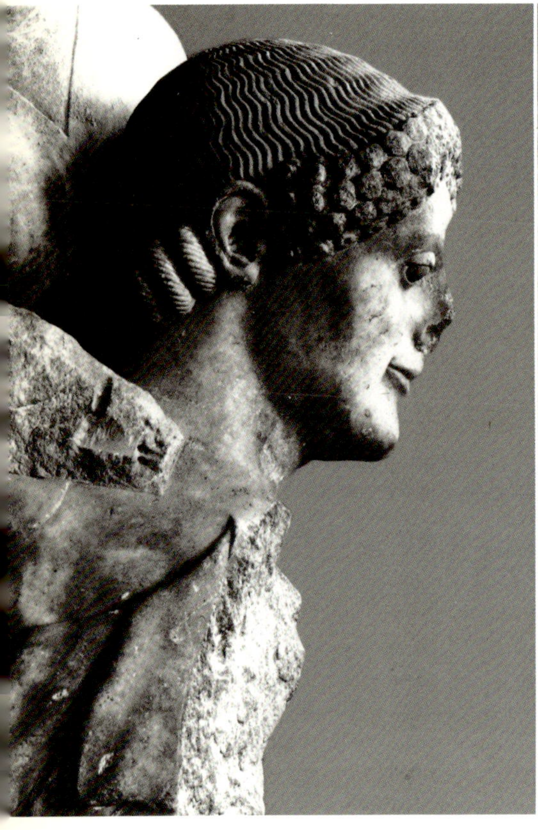

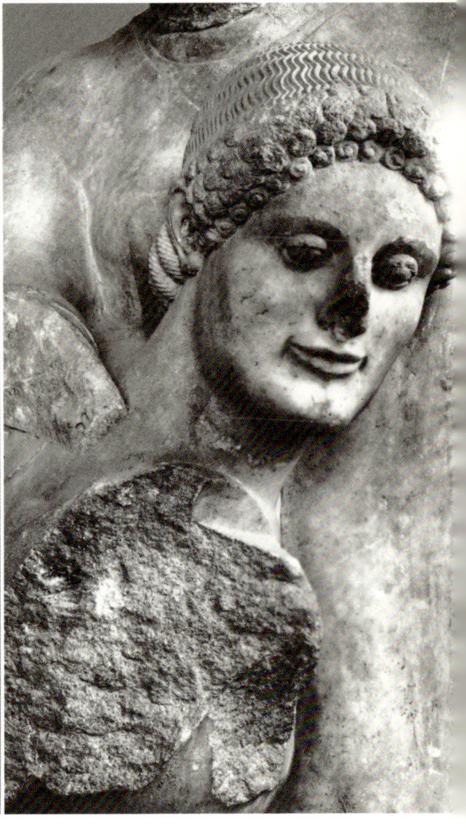

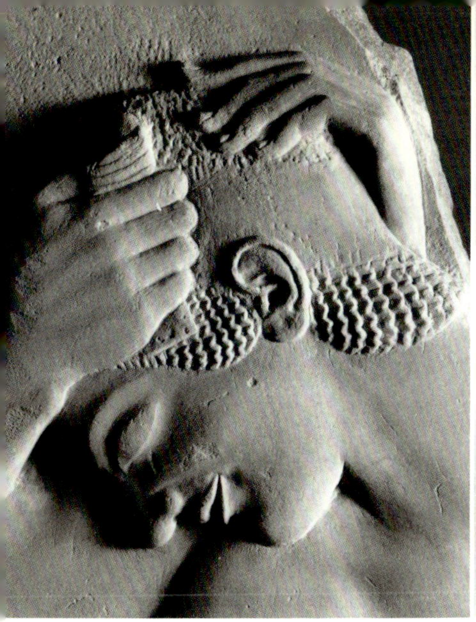

16. **Head of the dying man** on the Getty relief. The raking light shows the subtlety with which the surfaces were modeled.

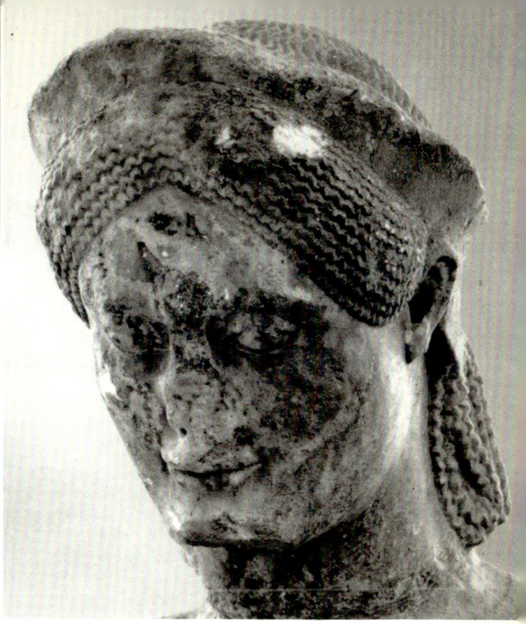

17. **Head of Antiope,** also from the pedimental sculptures of the temple of Apollo Daphnephoros (see also figs. 15, 56). Although much battered and encrusted, the finely carved features show a more delicate version of the dying youth on the Getty relief, including the same crimped hair style. Chalkis, Museum.

by Euphronios (fig. 20),[33] Herakles struggles with the mythological creature Antaios, the giant son of mother Earth. The hero is presented as if he has just left the hairdresser; his elaborate curls are rendered in dots of applied clay, much in contrast to the unkempt, scraggly hair of his opponent, which is loosely painted in diluted glaze. This disorderly hair is in keeping with Antaios' hirsute eyebrows and the raucous gasp of pain escaping from the fence of his teeth. Herakles, of course, wins the combat with an ease suitable to the immortal gods. Another example of the significance of hairdressing can be seen on a panel of one of the earliest red-figure drawings (fig. 21),[34] where Dike (Justice) slays Adikia (Injustice). The drawing is rather negligent, but it is clear that Dike is a graceful woman of proper upbringing, while uncombed Adikia, with aquiline nose, uncouth appearance, and her ungirdled dress revealing her naked thighs, is the opposite. Adikia is also horribly tattooed like a barbarian, with dotted circles on her arms and legs. Further confirming her low social status, she disgracefully screams her defeat from a wide open mouth. A third example[35] brings us from the

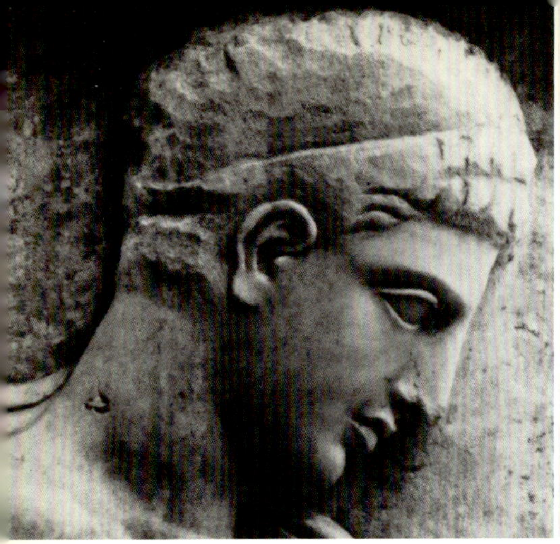

18. Grave relief of Eupheros. 430–420 B.C. The elaborately arranged hair was originally enhanced with gilding, traces of which could still be seen for a few months when excavated in 1959. Athens, Kerameikos Museum.

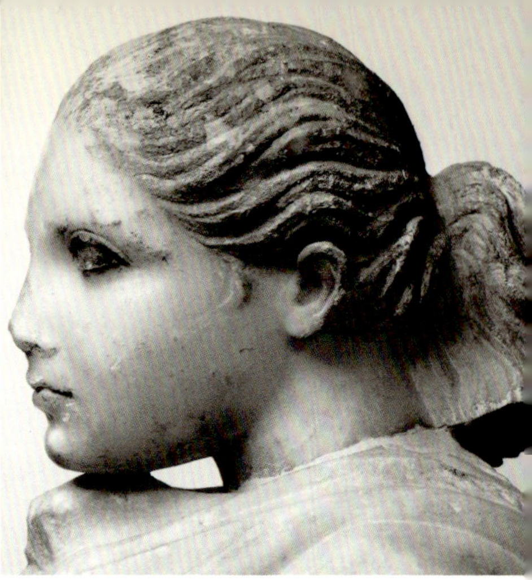

19. Head of a muse with gilded hair. Roman statue from ca. A.D. 200, after a Greek prototype. The original paint in the eyes and nostrils is also well preserved. Collection Hans Cohn, on loan to the J. Paul Getty Museum.

world of the gods and social allegory to everyday life in the *gymnasion.* On a skyphos painted by the Brygos Painter about 480 B.C. (fig. 22), athletes are training and maintaining the grounds with their hair beautifully arranged; among them is a small slave whose hair sticks out in all directions—the differentiation of social class is clear.

Perhaps the most revealing story from the fifth century about the significance of hair style is preserved by Herodotos.[36] On the eve of the battle at Thermopylai, the Great King of Persia, intrigued and impatient because of the inactivity of the Spartans, sent a spy toward the enemy's lines. The spy returned laughing: "The Spartans have gone mad. They are combing and pomading their hair." The King joined the hilarity until Demaratos, an exiled Spartan king who accompanied Xerxes' court on the expedition against Greece, exclaimed, "Do not laugh, o King. When the Spartans are ready to put their lives at stake, they beautify their heads." Our friends practiced the same custom.

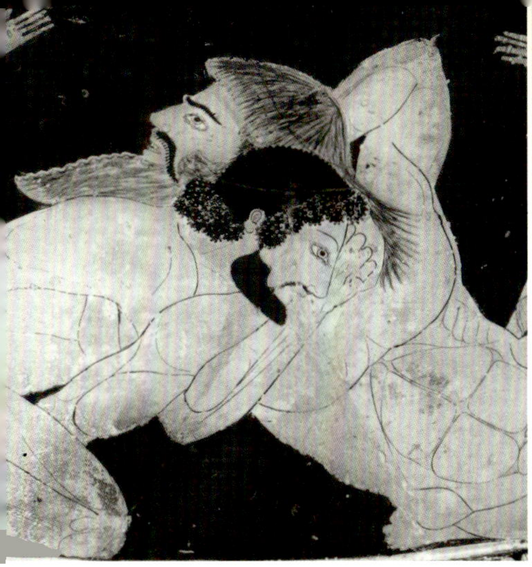

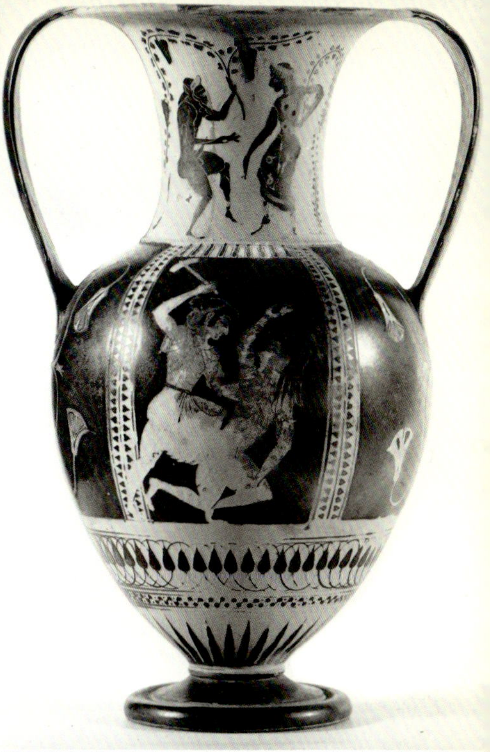

20. **The giant Antaios**, with shaggy beard and hair, being strangled by the well groomed hero Herakles. Detail of a calyx krater signed by Euphronios. Ca. 510 B.C. The curls of Herakles' hair style are not only painted but also modeled with tiny dots of applied clay.

21. **The elegant Dike (Justice)** slaying the unkempt Adikia (Unjustice). Bilingual neck amphora, ca. 525 B.C. Vienna, Kunsthistorisches Museum.

22. **Shaggy-headed and buck-toothed slave boy.** He attends immaculately groomed athletes. Ca. 480 B.C. by the Brygos Painter. The contrast between the boy's casual realism and the properly dignified rendering of the athletes reflects his low social status. Boston, Museum of Fine Arts. The James Fund and Special Contribution.

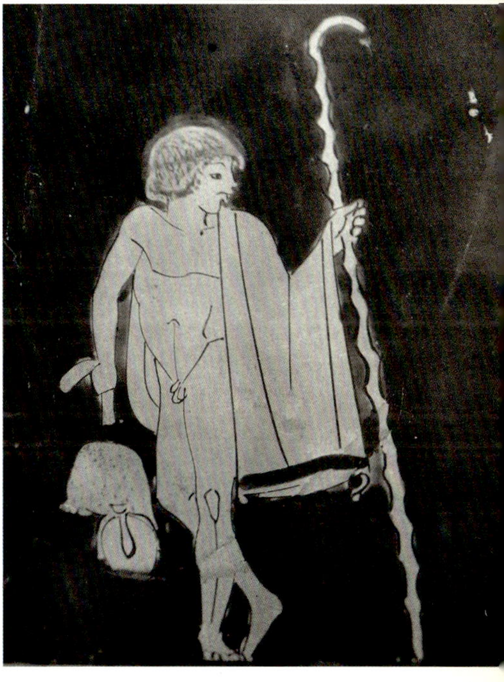

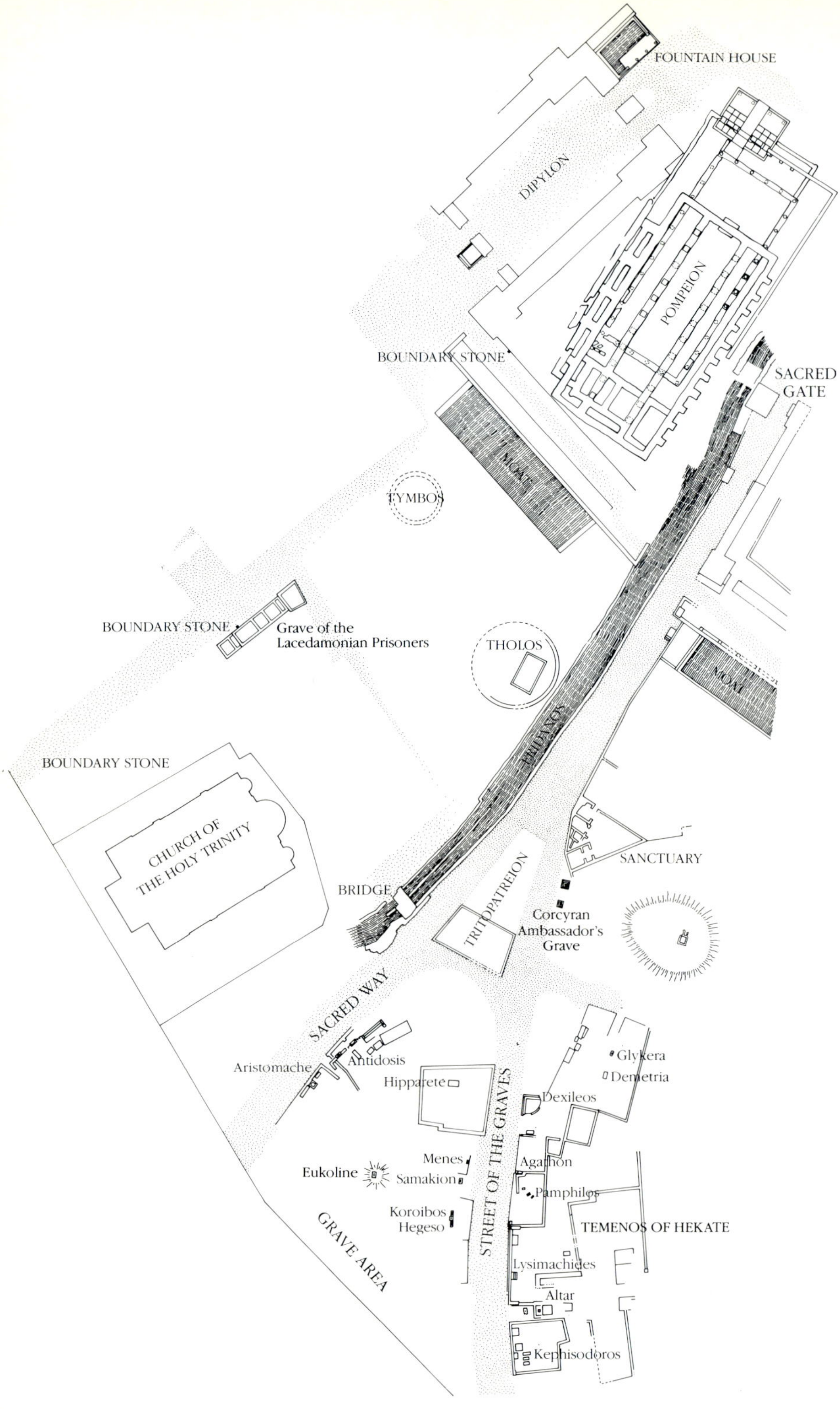
FOUNTAIN HOUSE
DIPYLON
POMPEION
BOUNDARY STONE
SACRED GATE
MOAT
TYMBOS
BOUNDARY STONE
Grave of the Lacedamonian Prisoners
THOLOS
MOAT
ERIDANOS
BOUNDARY STONE
CHURCH OF THE HOLY TRINITY
SANCTUARY
BRIDGE
TRITOPATREION
Corcyran Ambassador's Grave
SACRED WAY
Aristomache
Antidosis
Hipparete
STREET OF THE GRAVES
Glykera
Demetria
Dexileos
Menes
Eukoline
Samakion
Agathon
Pamphilos
Koroibos
Hegeso
TEMENOS OF HEKATE
GRAVE AREA
Lysimachides
Altar
Kephisodoros

Greek Funerary Monuments

From prehistoric times onwards, the Greeks marked burials with monuments.[37] During the Geometric period of the eighth century B.C., particularly on the grave of an aristocrat, a giant terracotta vase was placed next to a small stone marker, usually a roughly cut pilaster (fig. 24). These vases, decorated with funerary scenes, were half buried in the earth, and served simultaneously as the principal monument and as a receptacle for libations.[38] From the later seventh century B.C. onwards, stone memorials replaced these large vases.

Graves were placed outside the city and village settlements. In Athens the graves of the rich and famous were to be seen in two major locations: along the road leading out from the Sacred Gate toward Eleusis and on the parallel road leaving the famous Dipylon (double) Gate. This cemetery, traversed by the small creek Eridanos, is today called the Kerameikos[39] after the neighborhood (fig. 23). Systematic excavations of this cemetery began in the late nineteenth century and today still reveal the finest examples of Greek funerary art from all periods, starting from the dawn of the Mycenaean community and continuing until late Roman times. In the countryside of Attica, funerary plots were distinct areas within each settlement, the burials of dependents being grouped around the mound of the aristocratic leaders. The social status of the deceased and his family was revealed by the exuberance of the funeral ritual, the banquet for the participants,

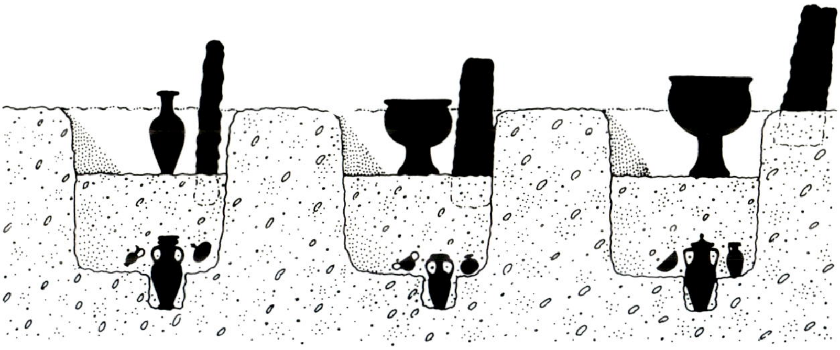

24. An Attic grave from the eighth century B.C., with colossal krater and stone marker. Drawing by Martha Breen Bredemeyer after Richter, *Gravestones,* p. 9.

23. Plan of the Kerameikos cemetery. Drawing by Martha Breen Bredemeyer after W. Hoepfner, *AM* 85 (1970) Beilage 5.

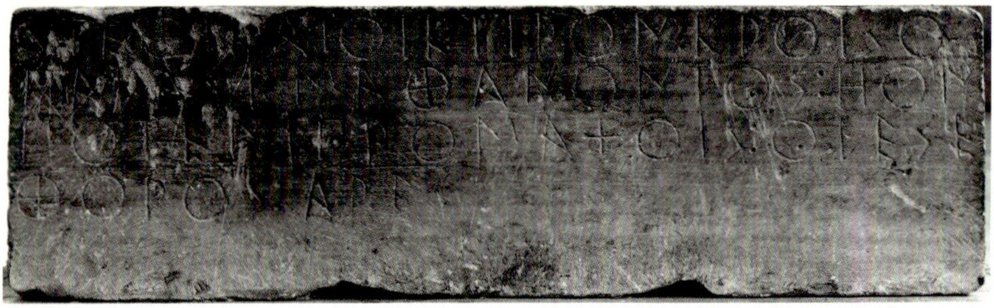

25. **Inscription** on the base of the statue of Kroisos (fig. 26).

the luxury of the grave offerings accompanying the deceased to the next world, and, of course, the size and richness of the funerary monument. Ostentatious funerals and monuments were often opportunities for arrogant aristocratic clans to parade themselves, provoking bloody brawls. Laws were repeatedly passed limiting the cost of these extravagant funerals, the number of people in the funerary procession, especially the women hired for lamentations, and also the cost of the monument. The first such sumptuary law, aimed against the hubris of Athenian aristocrats, is connected with Solon in the early sixth century.[40]

In the sixth century typical grave markings were statues or slabs of marble painted or carved with relief. We also find as funerary monuments both of the two basic types of archaic statuary—the *kouros* for men[41] and, less frequently, the *kore* for women.[42] Only the inscriptions distinguish them from the same types of statuary used as votive offerings. Kouroi sometimes represent Apollo, the young and beautiful god. The identification is easy when the statue carries a bow[43] and probable when a statue is found in a shrine of Apollo. More than forty kouroi can be traced to Delphi, but they were numerous in Delos and in other sanctuaries too.[44] It is not clear in every case whether the statue is intended as the god himself or as the votary presented in the image of the god or simply as a beautiful *agalma* (statue). The distinction may not always have been clear to the donor himself. The identity may be equally vague for kouroi representing victorious athletes or serving as funerary statues. The actual wording of the inscription is often limited to the name of the deceased, usually in the genitive case.[45] When a funerary inscription is extensive, it recalls the world of Homeric imagery and ideas. A good example is from the base of a funerary statue of a youth (figs. 25, 26) found in Anavysos,[46] the area from which the Getty relief also comes:

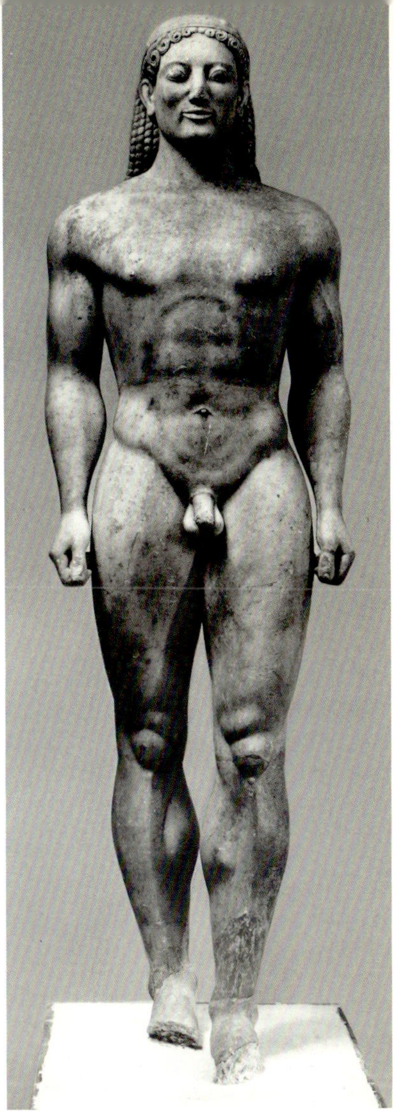

26. Funerary statue of Kroisos. From Anavysos; found in the same cemetery as the Getty relief. Ca. 530 B.C. The traditional pose, elaborate hair style, and ideal features are common to kouroi of the period. If the inscription naming Kroisos had not survived (fig. 25), it would be impossible to say whether the statue represented the god Apollo or a mortal man. Athens, National Museum.

> Stand and mourn before the grave sign of the departed
> Kroisos, who in the first rank of warriors,
> was destroyed by the furious Ares.[47]

Again, the idea of a beautiful death—*kalos thanatos*—echoes Homeric wording. The tradition remained strong in Greek culture, despite the fact that the nature of Greek warfare had changed utterly since Homer. From the seventh century onwards, battles were no longer exhibitions of heroic deeds by outstanding individuals but

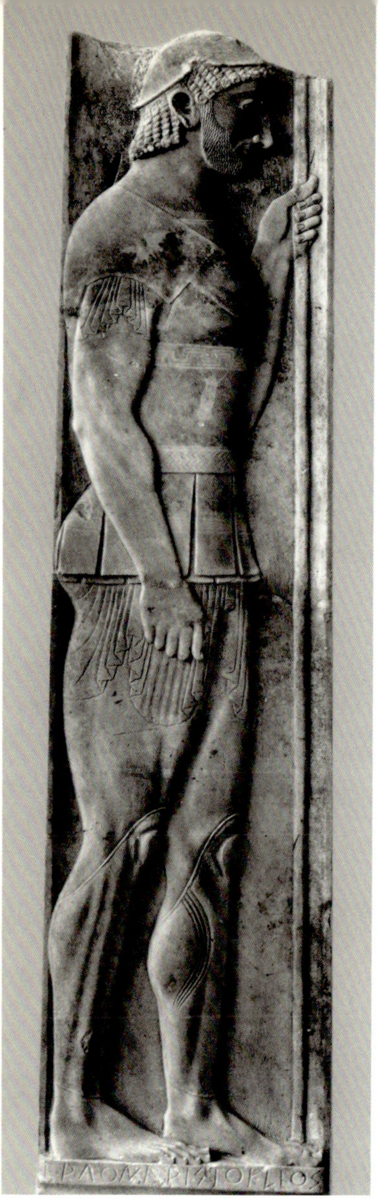

27. Grave stele of the Athenian Aristion. Signed by the sculptor Aristokles. Ca. 510 B.C. Aristion's depiction in full armor reflects the ideal of the aristocratic warrior code, ignoring the fact that the Homeric concept of the individual hero had been anachronistic for generations. Athens, National Museum.

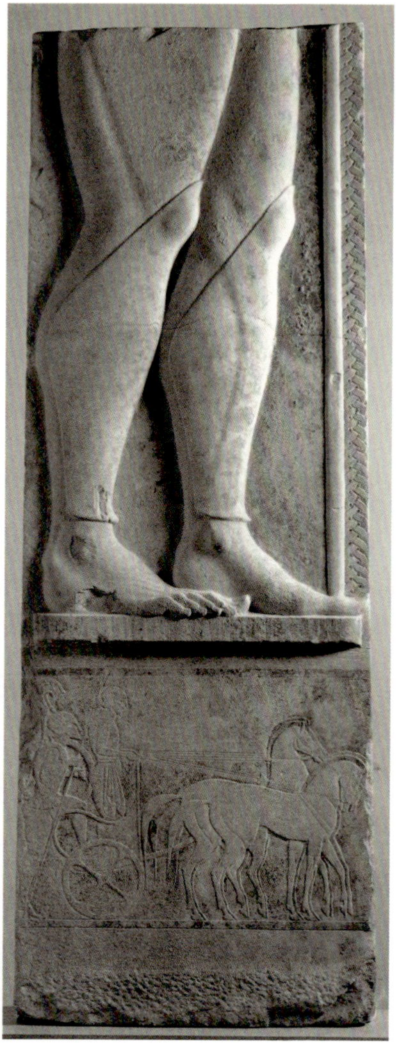

28. Lower part of the grave monument of an Attic warrior. Rich traces of the original polychromy survive. Ca. 530 B.C. The hero mounting his four-horse chariot is another survival of the Homeric ethos and not at all reflective of sixth-century battle tactics. New York, The Metropolitan Museum of Art, Fletcher Fund, 1938.

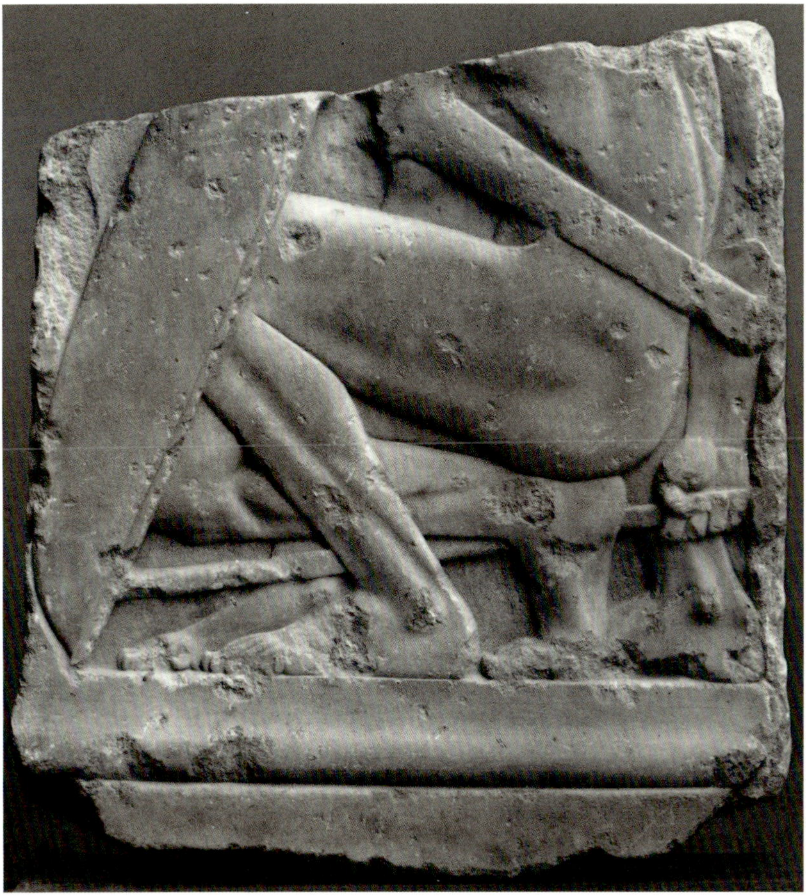

29. **Two warriors in profile,** the first kneeling protected by a round shield and the second standing behind. Fragment of an Attic grave stele. About 500 B.C. The two-figure composition, the complex pose of the kneeling warrior, and the probable interaction between the two warriors all relate this relief to the innovative climate around the Getty relief. Copenhagen, Ny Carlsberg Glyptotek.

rather clashes of heavily armed infantry aided by various auxiliaries. The success of a battle depended on good training and discipline. However, Kroisos is praised and represented like a Homeric hero, as were many of his fellows on contemporary grave monuments.

Parallel to the Homeric tradition, the iconographic repertory of funerary stelai in the archaic period was limited to two basic types—

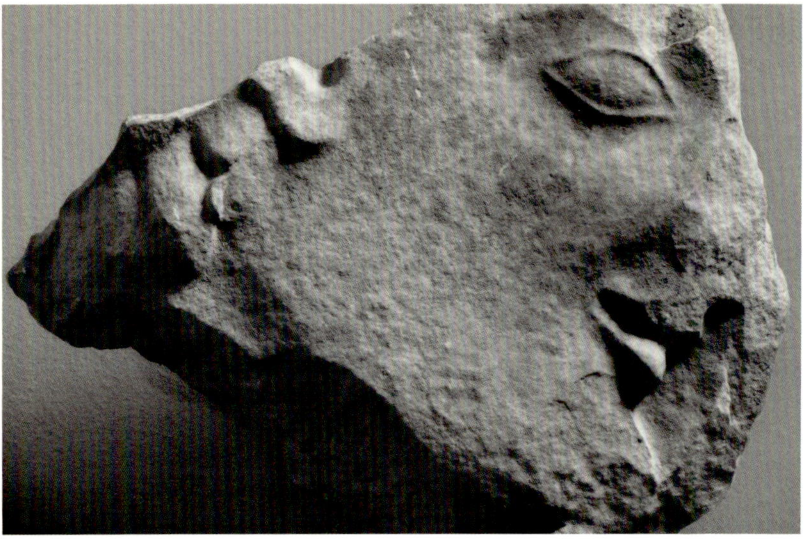

30. **Head of a youth.** Fragment of an Attic grave stele. Ca. 540 B.C. This much weathered and battered fragment predates the Getty relief by almost thirty years—witness the high cheekbone, everted contours of the eyes, and the unarticulated smile. Malibu, The J. Paul Getty Museum.

warriors and athletes. Representations of warriors were by far the most popular.[48] A good example is the inscribed grave stele in the Athens National Museum showing Aristion in full armor (fig. 27), signed about 510 B.C. by the sculptor Aristokles.[49] Another is the bottom fragment of a slightly earlier stele in the Metropolitan Museum of Art (fig. 28), showing the greaves of a standing warrior and a Homeric painted chariot scene underneath.[50] This monument preserves much of its original polychromy. Exceptionally, a scene of actual warfare, perhaps an ambush, is represented on a fragment from the very end of the sixth century if not from the first years of the fifth: two warriors are shown in profile; the first one kneels protected by a round shield, the other stands behind his companion (fig. 29).[51]

The second basic type represents the deceased as an athlete,[52] exceptionally as a victorious athlete with a crown[53] but normally with the attributes of sporting activities. A splinter of a relief from the first half of the sixth century in the Getty Museum[54] shows the now ruined but once radiant profile of a smiling youth (fig. 30); he may have been represented as an athlete. A superb fragment in the Athens National

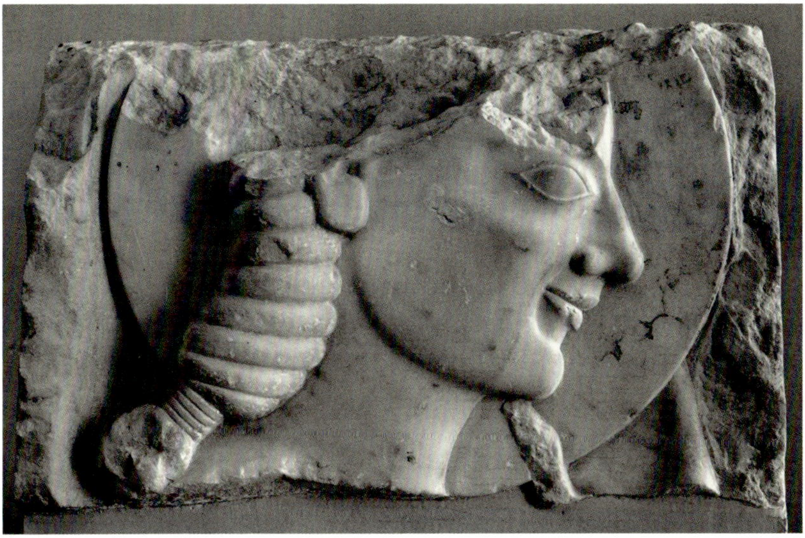

31. **Head of a youth carrying a discus.** Fragment of an Attic grave stele. Ca. 560 B.C. The use of the discus to frame the head of this young athlete with his immaculately coiffed hair shows superb compositional imagination within the limits of the iconography. Athens, National Museum.

Museum preserves the head of a youth with elaborately curled and braided hair (fig. 31);[55] the halo behind his head is nothing more than a discus, and the intention was to show the deceased youth in connection with the athletic discipline at which he presumably excelled. On another stele, also in the Metropolitan Museum (fig. 32),[56] a young man has an aryballos attached to his wrist. This perfume bottle, together with sponge and scraper, is the typical attribute of an athlete. The New York stele, dating ca. 530 B.C., departs from the standard iconography: a little draped girl is shown standing next to the nude youth, presenting a riddle of interpretation. The fragmentary inscription mentions the mother of the deceased, but the figure is too small for an adult. Is she his sister? Or is she small as an expression of the subordinate status of female figures, the whole world of the archaic grave stelai remaining exclusively male?

Even these few examples illustrate an essential aspect of archaic Attic grave reliefs: the artistic quality is consistently outstanding, and many are masterpieces. Still, very few reach the superb artistic level of the Getty piece.[57]

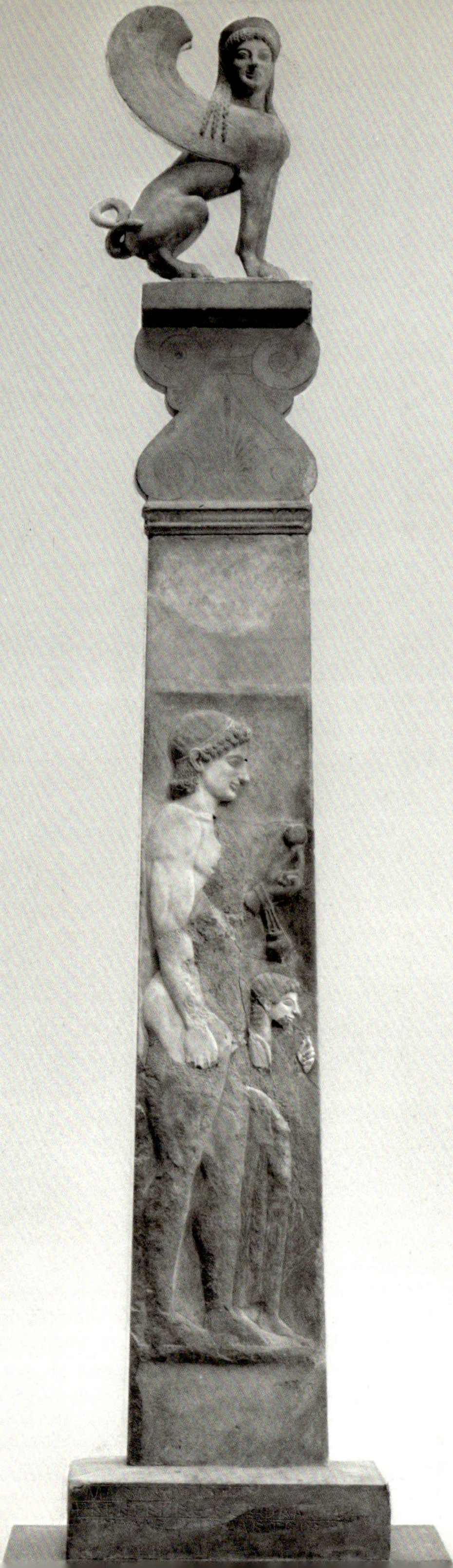

Funerary Stelai

The typical archaic Greek grave stele was made of a tall slab of marble. At the end of the seventh century and the beginning of the sixth, it was rather thick. Later it was cut thinner, about ten cm thick. Some of the earliest specimens are of limestone, but others are of marble which quickly became the standard material.[58]

Starting in the beginning of the sixth century, the marble stele was solidly anchored in a base of common stone hidden under the earth.[59] The stele itself was made in two parts. The finial was set into a cavity carved into the top of the main slab. During the first half of the century, this top usually culminated in a crouching sphinx.[60] An epigram on a Thessalian stele illustrates the funerary function of the creature:[61]

> O sphinx, dog of Hades, whom do you watch sitting over the dead?

By the late sixth century these figurative finials were replaced by intricate floral designs, most commonly an elaborate palmette that was sometimes accompanied by volutes and other decorative elements, often carved from the same marble slab as the figured relief. The proportions of the stele also changed, and the slab became wider.[62]

The production of archaic grave stelai in Attica ended in the early fifth century B.C. A reasonable explanation for this cessation is that the victorious democracy outlawed much of the ostentatious display of aristocratic pride. There may even have been a law specifically forbidding elaborate funerary monuments. The use of stelai continued, however, in other areas of Greece.[63]

In Athens grave stelai reappear in the late fifth century, during the last decade of the Peloponnesian War. The themes are completely different. Warriors sometimes appear (fig. 33),[64] but they are framed by other members of their families, among whom the women gain predominance. One might say that, instead of emphasizing the apotheosis of the military elite, the focus is on perpetuation of family bonds unit-

32. **A young athlete with a small-scale female.** Attic grave stele with a sphinx finial. 530–520 B.C. The small size of the woman may indicate that she is a servant or young sibling or may reflect the subordinate status of women in Athens, since the woman mentioned in the inscription is the mother. Most of the monument is in New York, The Metropolitan Museum of Art, Hewitt Fund, 1911; Rogers Fund, 1921; Munsey Fund, 1936 and 1938; Anonymous Gift, 1951. Plaster casts of three parts are preserved elsewhere: the front of the youth's chest and his flank are in Athens, National Museum, and the head of the girl is in Berlin.

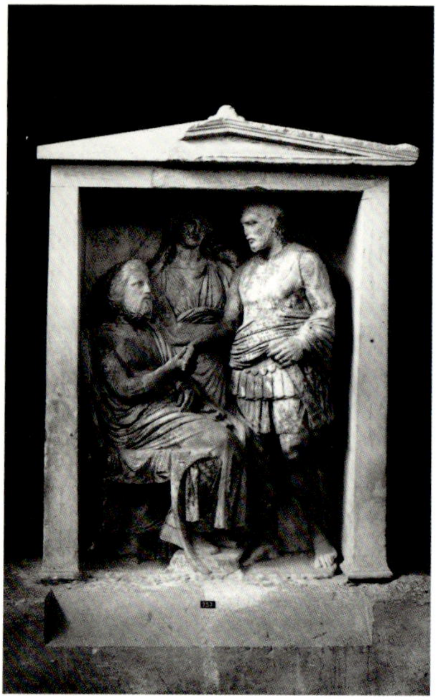

33. The dead Prokleides in full armor with his father and mother. Attic grave stele from 340–330 B.C. This late classical image combines the traditional depiction of the deceased as a warrior with a poignant scene of family leave-taking. Athens, National Museum.

ing the living with the dead across the border of the Underworld (fig. 34).[65] Unlike the archaic stelai, which were made for an aristocratic clientele, classical funerary monuments of the late fifth and fourth centuries were commissioned mostly by the Athenian middle class. And whereas in archaic times the workmanship had been uniformly high and masterpieces common, classical stelai were for the most part mass-produced, and sometimes even were intended for beloved house slaves. The end of the classical stele in its turn was likewise enacted by law, as promulgated by Demetrios of Phaleron, a student of philosophy and ruler of Athens by the grace of the Macedonian king whose interests he protected.[66] This law, preserved in Cicero,[67] stated:

> Nothing should be built above the mound of earth except a small column no more than three cubits high or a table or a small basin.

Demetrios ruled Athens from 317–310 B.C., and the anti-luxury law must have been passed toward the end of his rule. This date marks the end of the flourishing production of Attic grave reliefs,[68] although in the Attic countryside grave monuments continued to be erected for

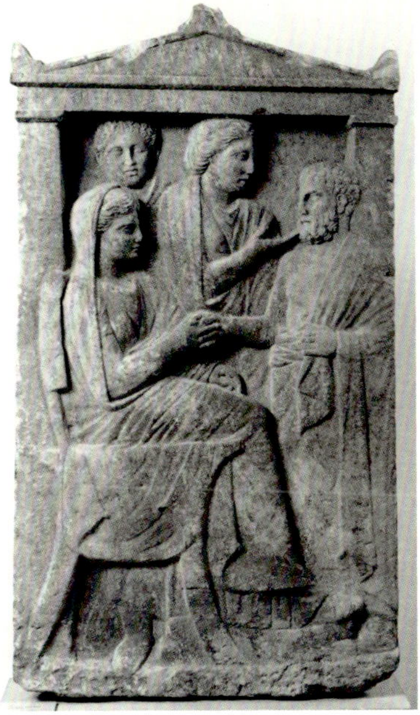

34. **Grave relief of Sime,** represented with all her family. Ca. 340–330 B.C. This rather crude relief uses all the conventional symbols—eye contact, handclasp, beard touch, frontal background figure—to convey the family's grief at the loss of the seated woman. Malibu, The J. Paul Getty Museum.

another decade or so. In other parts of the Greek world, funerary monuments continued to be produced throughout the Hellenistic period, with a new flowering in the second century B.C. (fig. 35).[69] During Roman domination, they reappear even in Athens (fig. 36).[70]

The Getty relief is exceptional among funerary stelai in three ways. First, its subject is unique. Second, its dimensions and shape are large; and, moreover, compared with the usually tall and narrow pieces, very wide. Third, the strong expression of emotions has hardly any parallel in archaic art. To some extent, a relief in Athens (fig. 37) may be compared to the unusual Getty piece. Variously interpreted by archaeologists as either funerary or votive, it represents a *hoplitodromos,* a youth running in armor, a theme that unites both basic types of funerary iconography. The relief is also exceptionally wide and rather large.[71] Dated about 510 B.C., it is contemporary with the Getty relief. Another relief in Athens, representing a mother and deceased child (figs. 6, 51),[72] must also have had unusual proportions. Its subject is also remarkable, and the relationship of the two figures, with the mother supporting the child's head with her left hand, is related to the Getty relief not only by its composition but also by its strong emotional content. The affinity

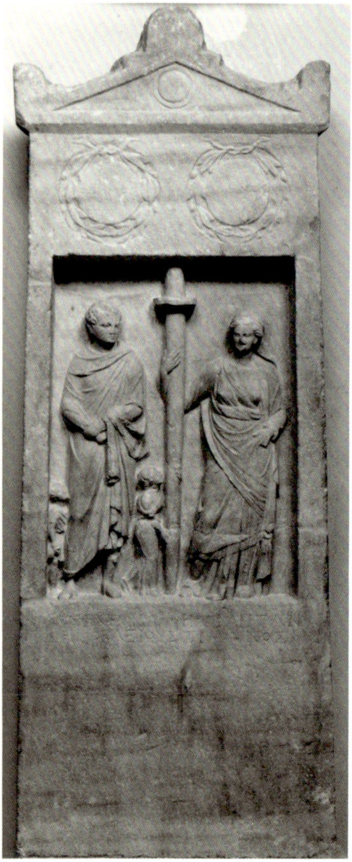

35. Grave relief of Posideos and Herophanta. From Smyrna. Second century B.C. Both poses reflect major sculptural types of the age—philosopher and priestess. The crowns indicate that they were honored by their city; it is not certain whether this was truth or fiction. Malibu, The J. Paul Getty Museum.

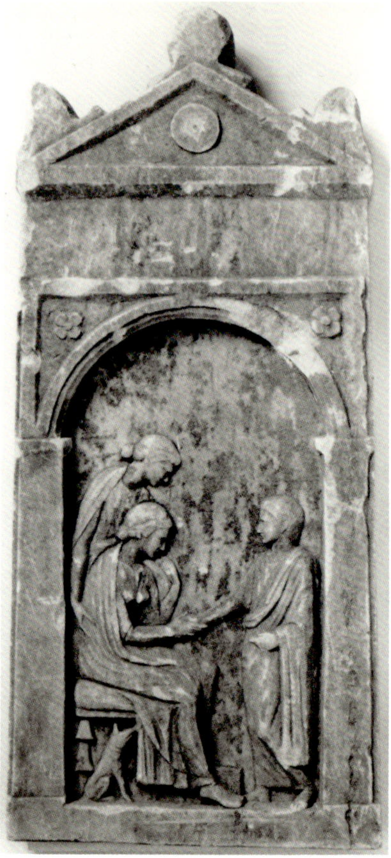

36. Grave stele of a boy represented with his mother and sister and his pet dog. The relief from the early first century A.D. intentionally follows in subject, spirit, and carving classical fourth-century B.C. Greek prototypes. Malibu, The J. Paul Getty Museum.

of the two reliefs goes further: it does not require close examination to see that both reliefs were created by the same artist, even if not at the same time.

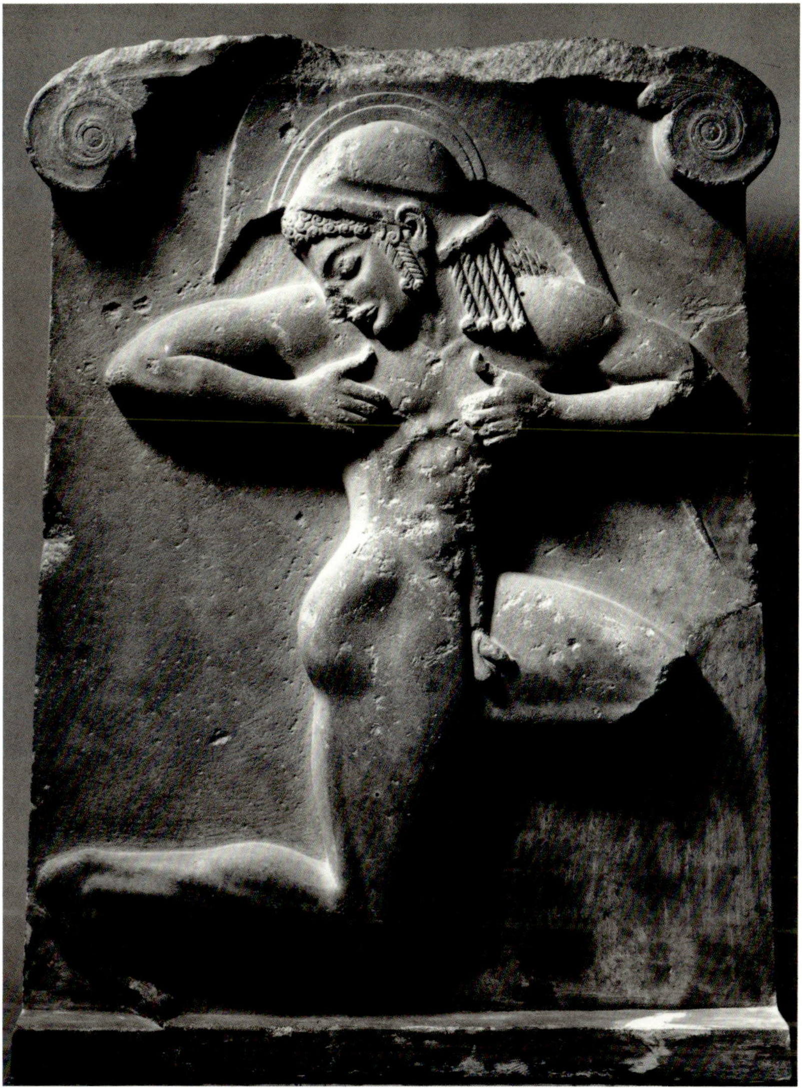

37. **Athlete running in armor.** Attic funerary (?) monument. Ca. 510 B.C. In the race in armor, competitors wore helmets and shields, symbolic of their wartime civic obligation. The exaggerated pose to indicate running, the everted head, and the strained combination of profile and frontal views must reflect earlier traditions. Athens, National Museum.

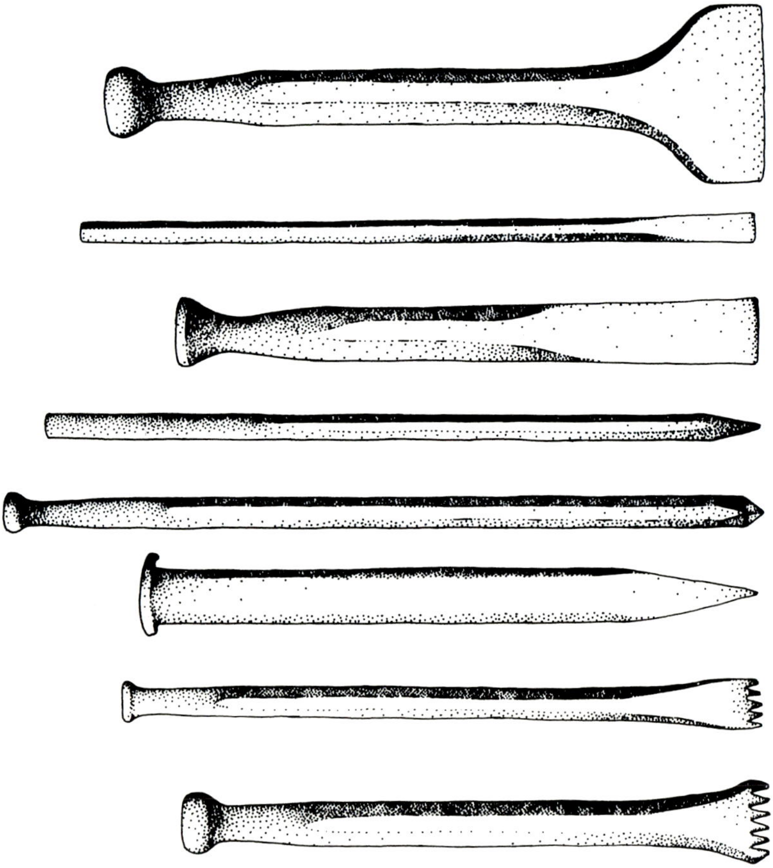

38. Sculptors' tools. Top to bottom: flat chisels, punches, claw chisels. Drawing by Martha Breen Bredemeyer after G. M. A. Richter, *The Sculpture and Sculptors of the Greeks* (New York, 1970) fig. 480.

Carving a Stele

Work on a funerary relief began in the quarry where a marble block of appropriate size was liberated from the rock. It was cut with the grain running from top to bottom, so that the block could easily be freed from the rock with chisel and water-swollen wedges of wood, and following the natural slope of the quarry to ease the sliding of the block toward the harbor. Before shipping, the shape of the slab would have been defined more exactly, leaving the unnecessary ballast on shore. Someone from the sculptor's workshop, perhaps the master himself, must have taken part in the work at the quarry, supervising not only the shaping of the block but also checking that there were no flaws or cracks in the layers of marble which could destroy the work during any of the next stages.[73]

In the workshop the block was roughly shaped with a pick, traces of which can be seen on the back of the Getty slab even in its finished state (fig. 38). The front, sides, and top edges were then planed smooth with a claw chisel. The sides of the Getty relief retain traces of this tool as they were never finely polished (fig. 39). Along the top of the Getty piece the sculptor then made two small cavities, too small to hold a major tenon of marble. The finial of the stele, carved from a separate slab of marble, must have been held in place by small metal (bronze) pins held firmly in position by lead poured into these small cavities. The front of the block was then polished with a flat chisel.

Only after this preparation did the sculptor make a rough drawing of his figural scene on the front of the slab. He may have used charcoal, but he probably incised some light guidelines in the stone. On the Getty relief, a guideline can be seen under the protruding top of the slab (fig. 40); it marked the lower edge of the painted molding ornament, now completely vanished. The stele in the Louvre created by the same artist (fig. 41) preserves these engraved lines, intended only as a guide for painting; some of the drapery folds (intended to be only painted) were omitted from the schematic incisions. Afterwards, the sculptor proceeded with the actual carving of the relief. Using a flat chisel which he held in his right hand and hit with a mallet held in his left, the sculptor cut progressively into the surface. This way of working remained in use throughout most of antiquity, whether the craftsman was left-handed or, less appropriately for this position of the instrument, right-handed. This means that the right contour of the

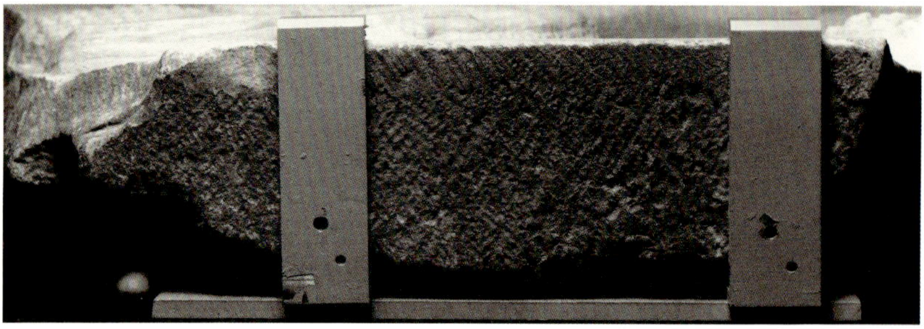

39. **The marks of the claw chisel** on the top of the Getty relief.

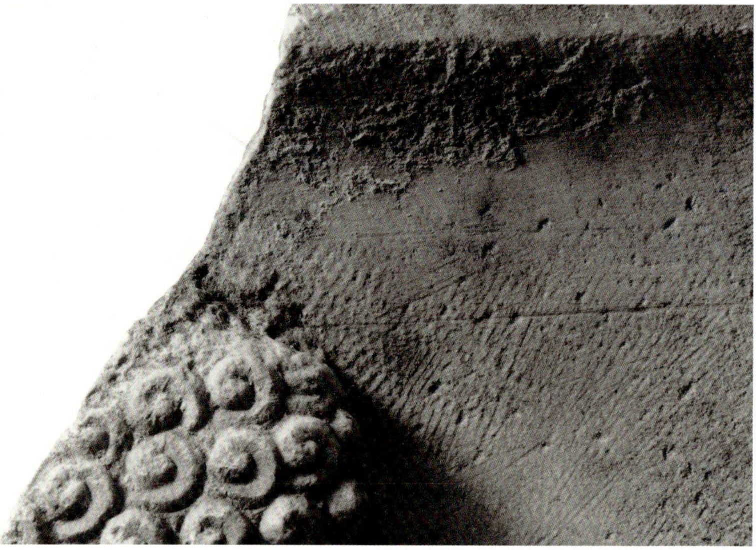

40. **Note the lightly incised guideline** under the top of the Getty relief, with traces of the flat chisel in the background.

relief figures is never so perfectly defined as the left side. However, a well-trained craftsman was able to achieve a consistent, flat level in the background; in later times, especially in the mass-produced grave reliefs of the fourth century, the plane of the background often remains uneven. Some details were continued with the edge of the chisel, and the surface was cleaned with a scraper. Finally, the sculpted surfaces, especially the nude parts of the human body, were polished

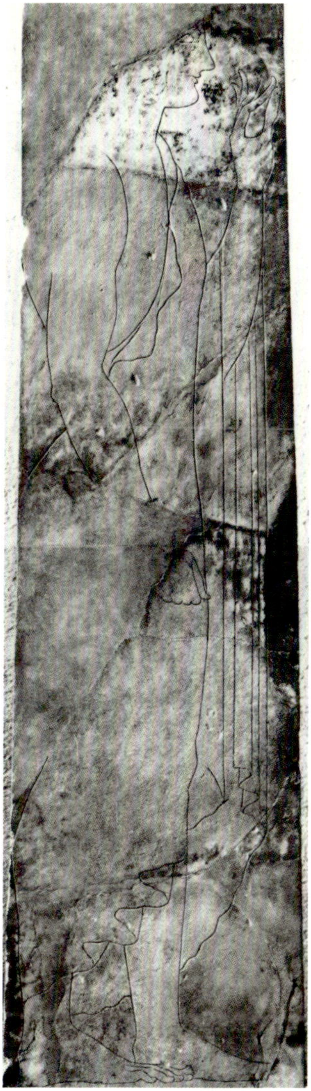

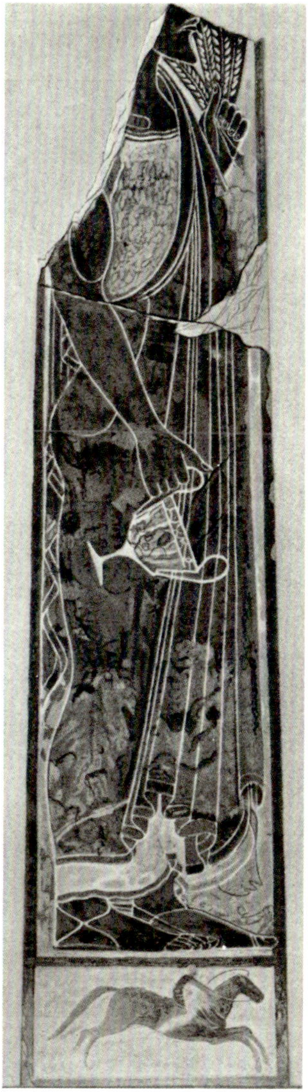

41. **Attic engraved stele of a youth**. 520–510 B.C. The deeply incised contour lines, vibrant with strength and vitality, originally guided the areas of color application—a powerful combination of relief sculpture and painting. Paris, Musée du Louvre.

42. **Reconstruction drawing of the stele of Lyseas the Athenian**. 510–500 B.C. The original is now mostly faded, but the painted contours and broad areas of color were clear on excavation in the nineteenth century. Athens, National Museum.

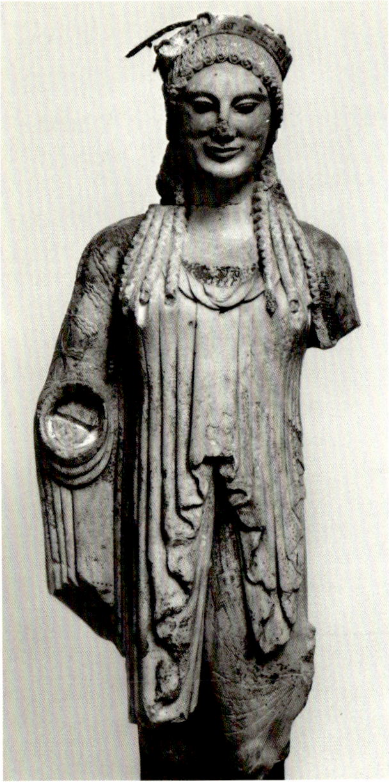

43. **Statue of a girl** dedicated on the Athenian Acropolis. 520–510 B.C. Athens, Acropolis Museum.

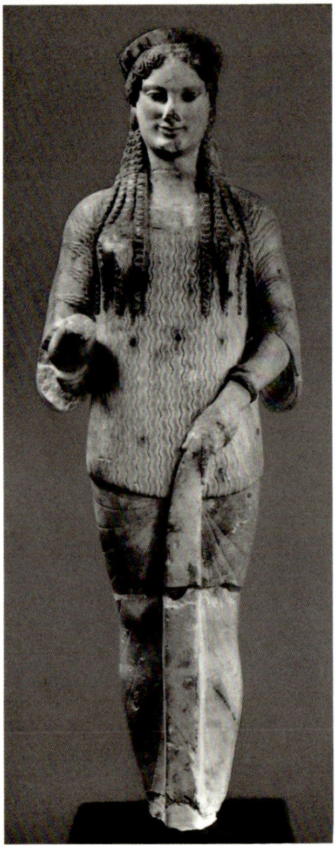

44. **Statue of a girl** from the Athenian Acropolis akin to fig. 43 but by a different sculptor. Athens, Acropolis Museum.

with marble powder mixed with some liquid.[74]

The final stage was painting.[75] All ancient Greek sculpture had rich polychromy. On a relief, polychromy enhanced the close relationship to wall painting. The predella of the archaic grave stele in the Metropolitan Museum of Art[76] (fig. 28), compared with the painted stele of Lyseas in the Athens National Museum (fig. 42) or the engraved and painted stele in the Louvre (fig. 41)[77], illustrates the point. Perhaps already in this early period, gilding was used for some details. While the background was usually painted blue, the prevailing color was red, used not only for lips and thinned for the cheeks but also for hair (sometimes as a base for gilding) and even for eyes.[78]

The Sculptor of the Getty Relief

The Getty Museum relief is an exceptional masterpiece. The subject, the bandaging of a mortally wounded man, is rare in Greek art and nonexistent in surviving monuments of sculpture. The interactive composition of two figures has only one parallel in archaic art, the stele of a mother and child (fig. 6),[79] the only other surviving monument of archaic sculpture that expresses emotion with such intensity. Even so, the mortal agony in the Getty relief is suggested rather than explicitly depicted, just as, a decade earlier, the great vase painter Exekias had drawn Ajax desperately alone and preparing for suicide with similar restraint.[80] The uniqueness of the Getty relief is easily explained by the fact that it is a masterpiece created by a great artist. His name may remain forever unknown, but his personality and career can nonetheless be traced amid the surviving monuments of archaic Attic sculpture.

Such an identification proceeds by comparing and examining sculptures in detail. The way *not* to proceed is to start with similar external features or even with identical motifs. The sculptors of ancient Athens looked very closely at each other's work and were quick to adopt any successful new technical detail or artistic motif. Their primary aim was not to create something novel and original. Rather, they repeated traditional, well-established themes from a stock repertoire and sought to do them better. This apparently traditional approach nevertheless permitted considerable innovation in artistic procedures. The easiest way to demonstrate the process of attribution of sculptures to the hands of a particular artist is to discuss some examples.

Two korai from the Athenian Acropolis, both dating after 520 B.C., are traditionally associated and have even been attributed by several scholars to the same sculptor. The heads are indeed similar, but even a casual look at the bodies excludes the possibility that the same hand was involved. One of the korai (fig. 43)[81] wears the traditional archaic pattern of drapery folds, while the other's dress, treated like a sweater adhering to her body (fig. 44),[82] emphasizes her more juvenile appearance. She is gauche to the point of being touching and has not yet outgrown her puppy fat. The superficial similarity of the two korai may be easily explained by the fact that, in general conception, each in a different way descends from the masterpiece that is the Peplos Kore (fig. 46),[83] carved a decade earlier. The softness of their faces and their

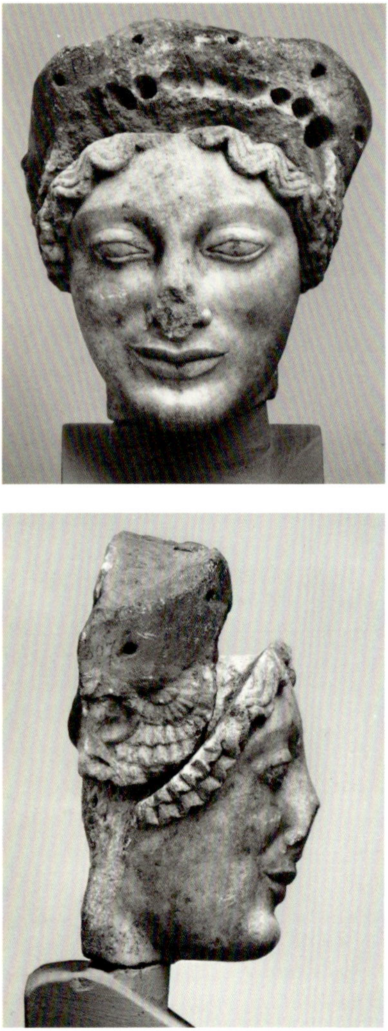

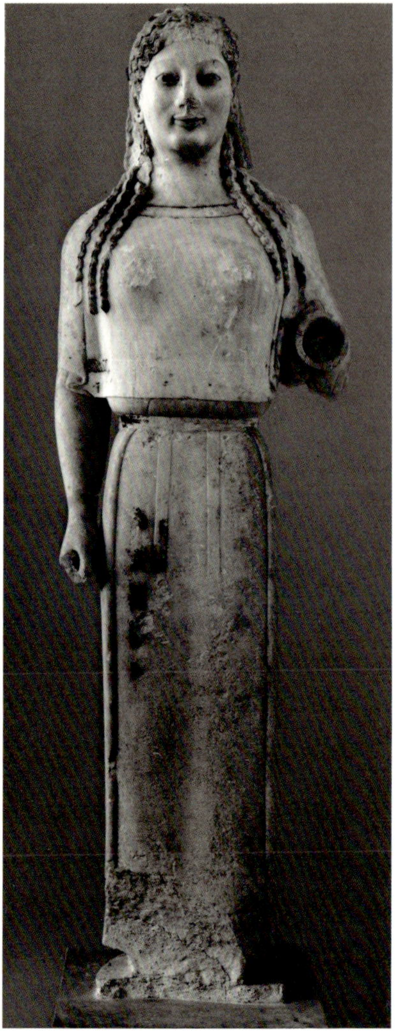

45. **Head of a girl** dedicated on the Athenian Acropolis. Ca. 520 B.C. It is called the Payne head after the English archaeologist H. Payne who recognized its quality as a masterpiece. Athens, Acropolis Museum.

46. **Statue of a girl** dedicated on the Athenian Acropolis. The so-called Peplos Kore. Ca. 530 B.C. Athens, Acropolis Museum.

sweet, inscrutable smiles also owe much to another masterpiece, also from the Athenian Acropolis, the unforgettable fragment called the Payne head (fig. 45).[84] The obvious relationship with the Payne head has even generated the hypothesis that it, a unique masterpiece, may be attributed to the same hand as the two korai. All these attributions must be rejected; they are based on similarities of motif, while the style and the execution of these four sculptures are radically different.

Another example concerns two reliefs depicting the same subject, the earlier of which is connected stylistically with the Getty relief. On one side of a well-preserved relief base for a funerary kouros, found near the Kerameikos in 1920 and now in the National Museum of Athens, is depicted a ball game (fig. 48).[85] Two of the figures on its right side survive on a fragmentary relief, recently discovered in the Kerameikos (fig. 47) and now in the Kerameikos Museum.[86] The Kerameikos relief was reused in a late antique construction, and most of the carved face has been destroyed. Judging from the surviving parts, the compositions of both reliefs were identical down to the last detail, including the ingenious view of the bearded figure, who is seen from behind with his left foot raised, allowing the sole of his foot to appear. The surface of the complete base in the Athens National Museum suffered from slight recutting very soon after its original carving, probably in order to repair some damage.[87] Even so, it is evident that the original carving of the two bases was different. The Kerameikos Museum base is considerably superior, and the carving dates some years prior to the other. The comparison emphasizes once more that originality was not the primary concern of Greek artists. While to do better was the true Greek spirit, the second attempt was sometimes the work of a less competent craftsman following the courageous lead of a master.

The artist of the relief in the Kerameikos Museum, who was the better sculptor,[88] is the same as the sculptor of the Getty relief. A group of six works by his hand is assembled here, spanning a career of over thirty years. His style is immediately apparent in certain details. He was particularly fascinated with the rendering of fingers. Their articulation and the gestures of the hands are indicated with a sensitivity that instantly brings to mind both the left hand of the mother cradling the head of her child in the fragmentary grave relief mentioned above (figs. 6, 51)[89] and the delicate fingers of the left hand of the youth on the Getty grave stele (fig. 16). (The fingers of the Theseus-Antiope group were retouched by a later—perhaps first-century B.C.—restoration.)

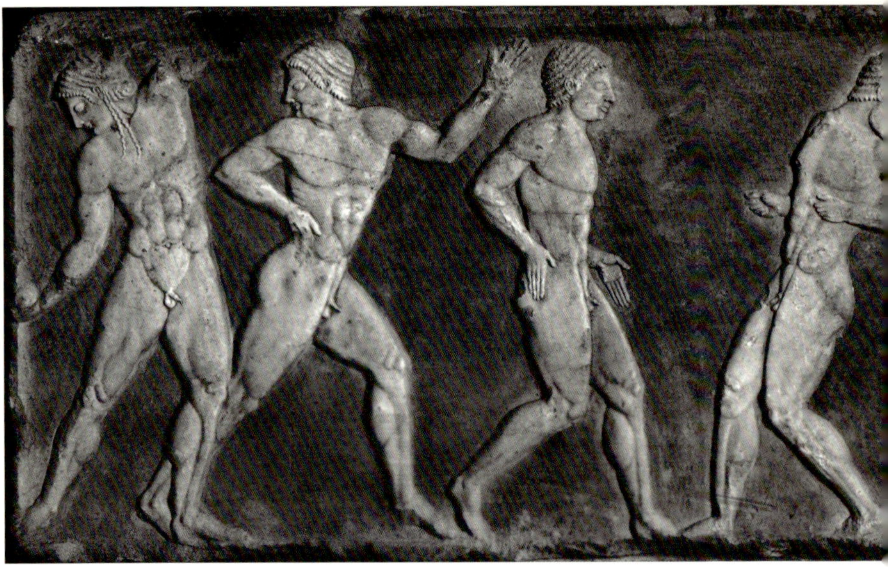

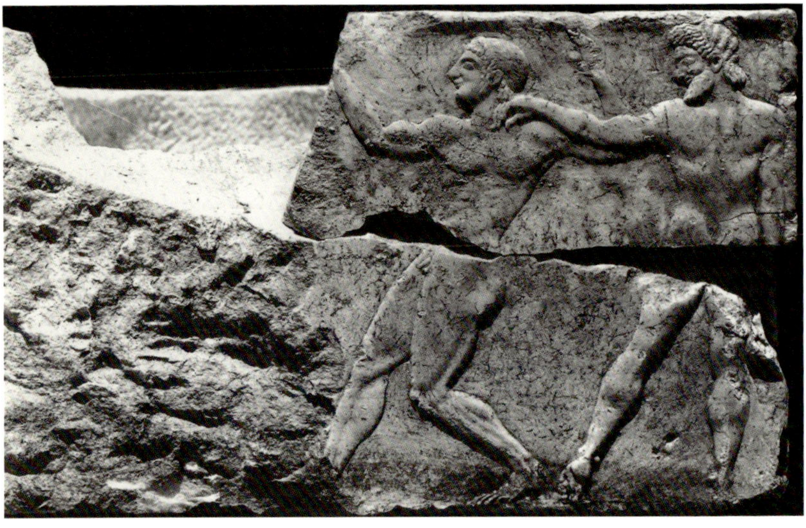

47. **Athletes playing a ball game**. Fragment of a relief on a base for a funerary statue of a youth. From the Kerameikos cemetery. By the same hand as the Getty relief. Athens, Kerameikos Museum.

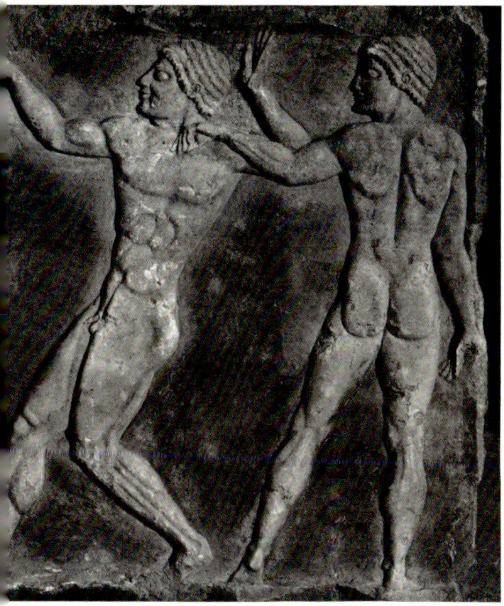

48. **Base with the same subject as fig. 47.** This is a replica, as the two right figures show. The poses are identical, although details of hair style, gesture, and proportion vary slightly. Athens, National Museum.

A German archaeologist has already compared the profile of the child with the head of the ephebe from the Kerameikos base.[90] The head of the child and the remains of the mother's profile show close parallels with both faces on the Getty relief (figs. 50 and 51), although the heads of the two youths exhibit considerably more anatomically unified features and the transitions from one group of muscles to another are much softer and less abrupt. Moreover, the child and the Getty youths share the same pouting lips, carved with vertical depressions at the corners; protruding chins; interrupted nasolabial lines forked toward the cheekbones; and circular, buttonlike nostrils. Finally, the articulation of the ears is very characteristic and recurs not only on these four heads but also on all other sculptures attributed to the hand.

The same stylistic features appear in the group of Theseus abducting Antiope from the pediment of the temple of Apollo Daphnephoros in Eretria (fig. 56) on the island of Euboia.[91] Here, the skill in rendering the anatomy is more advanced, but the style is identical. One detail, already mentioned, strengthens the kinship of the pediment with the Getty relief: while Theseus' curls mirror the hair style of the younger man (cf. figs. 53, 54), the spiky hair of Antiope corresponds to the head of his dying companion (figs. 17 and 10).

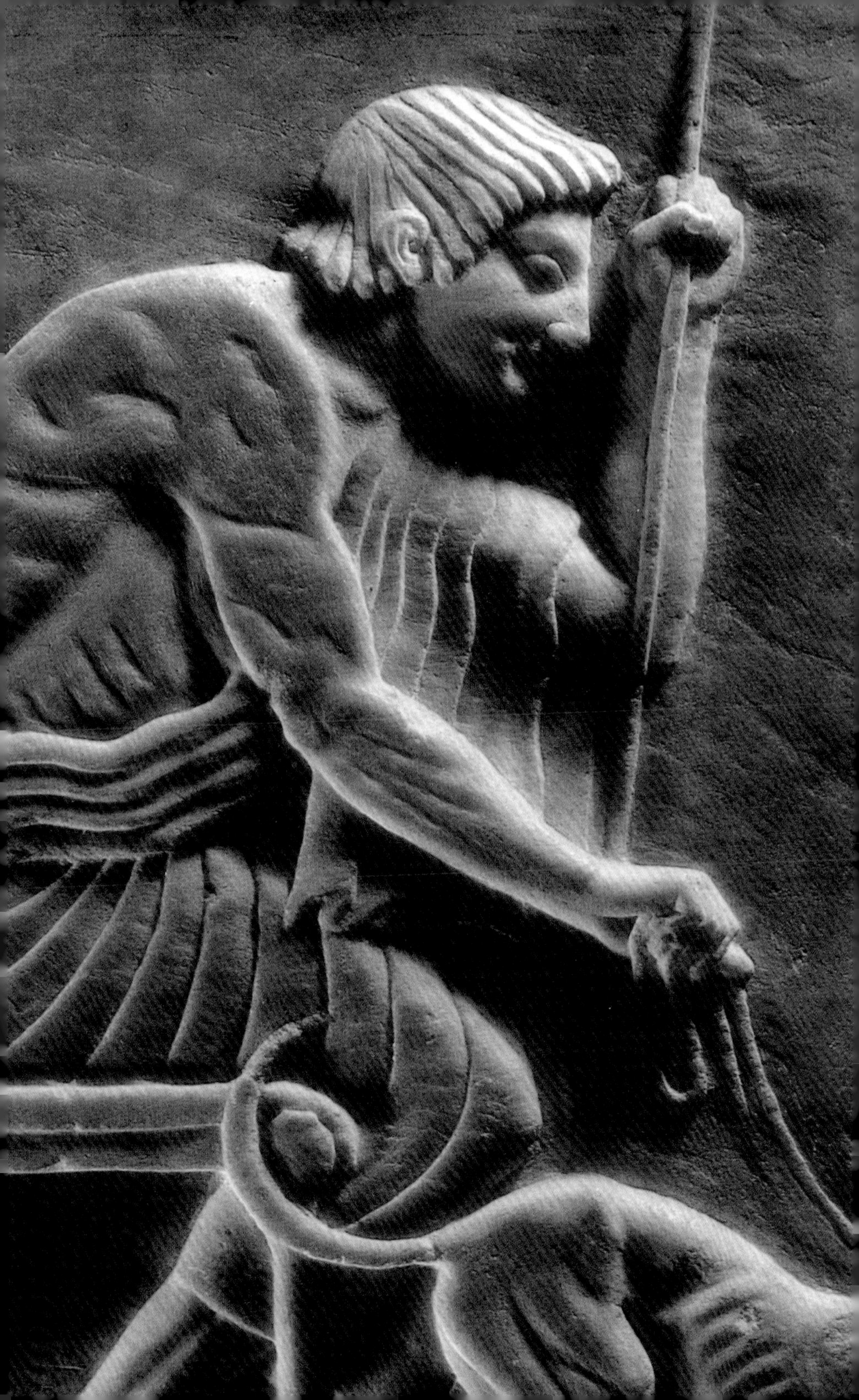

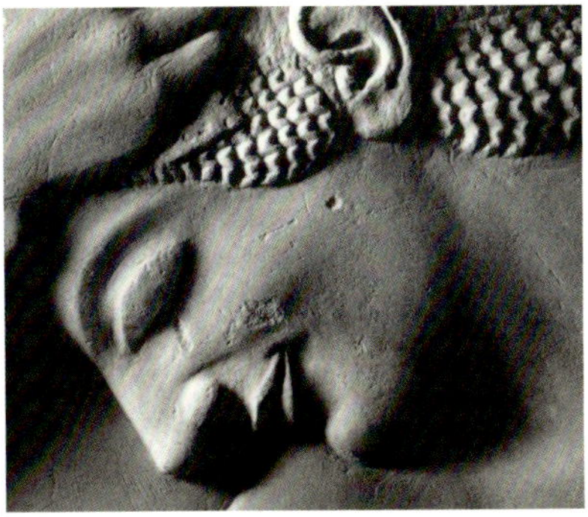

50. The dying man on the Getty relief.

A torso of an independent kouros (fig. 57)[92] is exhibited in the Chalkis Museum close to the Theseus and Antiope group. Direct visual comparison (although difficult with the available reproductions) leaves no doubt that both were carved by the same man. The torso is so close to the Theseus that it looks like his brother and suggests how the bodies of the Getty fragment may have looked, especially the more mature body of the dying man.

Finally, a piece that at first glance appears to be of a completely different nature must be discussed: an archaic grave stele from Anavysos and now in the Louvre, which was originally painted (figs. 41, 55).[93] The colors have vanished, but most of the lines engraved to guide the application of the color remain. A youth in profile holds what was probably a flower, originally painted and now vanished without trace, close to his nostrils in his long, sensitive fingers. His profile (fig. 55) corresponds closely to the face of the younger man on the Getty relief (fig. 54). Comparison of the two is more eloquent than any verbal analysis.

Considering the assembled group of six sculptures together, it is evident that the stele of the mother and child (fig. 6) is the most old-fashioned.[94] Compared with it, the young athlete from the Kerameikos base (fig. 52) seems a little more anatomically advanced, but both correspond to the first products of the red-figure technique in vase painting[95] and thus both date about 525 B.C., the relief perhaps a little later. The Getty gravestone belongs to the decade 520–510 B.C. Profiles of

49. Detail of another side of fig. 48, showing recutting done soon after erection of the base that is especially noticeable in the anatomical articulation, which has become sharp and jagged.

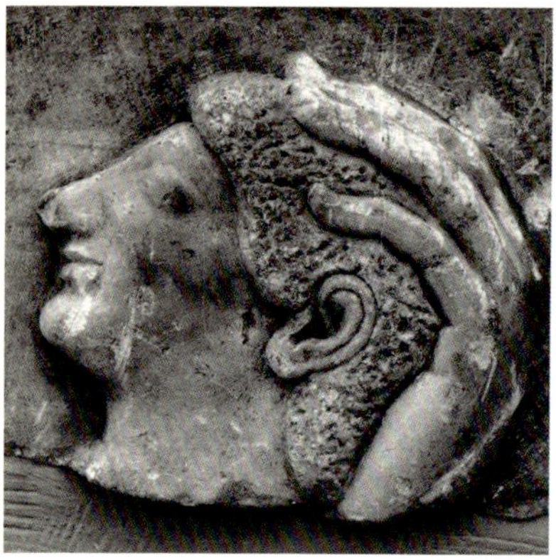

51. **Head of dead child** (detail of fig. 6).

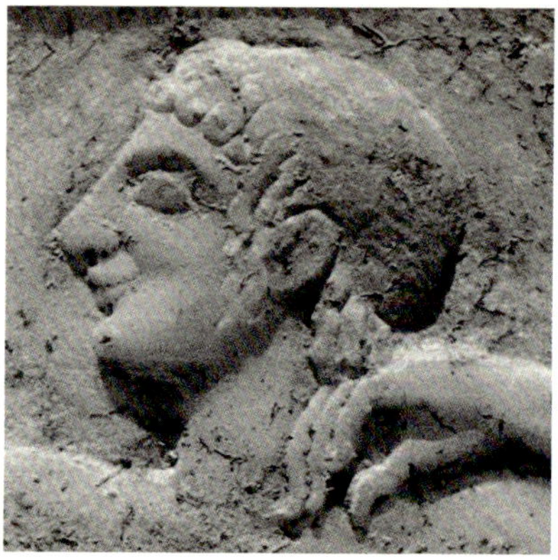

52. **The head of an athlete** from the Kerameikos base (detail of fig. 47).

youths comparable to the Getty relief heads exist among the drawings from the early career of the vase painter Oltos,[96] who specialized in the decoration of cups and was the teacher of the famous Euphronios. The engraved stele in the Louvre (fig. 41) has already been compared with the work of Euphronios and, even more, with the work of his fellow Pioneer vase painter, Phintias[97] (fig. 58[98]). Thus a date of circa 510 or slightly later must be correct. The group of Theseus and Antiope from the Eretria pediment (fig. 56) is universally dated about 510.[99] It follows the stage in the career of the great vase painter Euphronios represented by the signed calyx krater in the Metropolitan Museum of Art (fig. 13),[100] which has been convincingly dated before 510 B.C. The kouros in the Chalkis Museum (fig. 57) is the latest known work of our master, and it finds an appropriate place among other kouroi known from the same period.[101]

We do not know the name of the sculptor. He signed his work on the pediment of Eretria, but unfortunately only the verb "made" survives, while the name is irretrievably lost.[102] What is evident is that he was an outstanding master. He did not seek to innovate in details, in which he is rather traditional. Even in the later stages of his career, as characterized by the Louvre engraved stele, he enjoyed carving the representation of a youth sniffing a flower very much in the slightly mannered spirit of the preceding decade.[103] However, his hallmark is grandiose style. His solidly built and robust figures hark back to the Attic tradition of such great artists as the anonymous Master of the

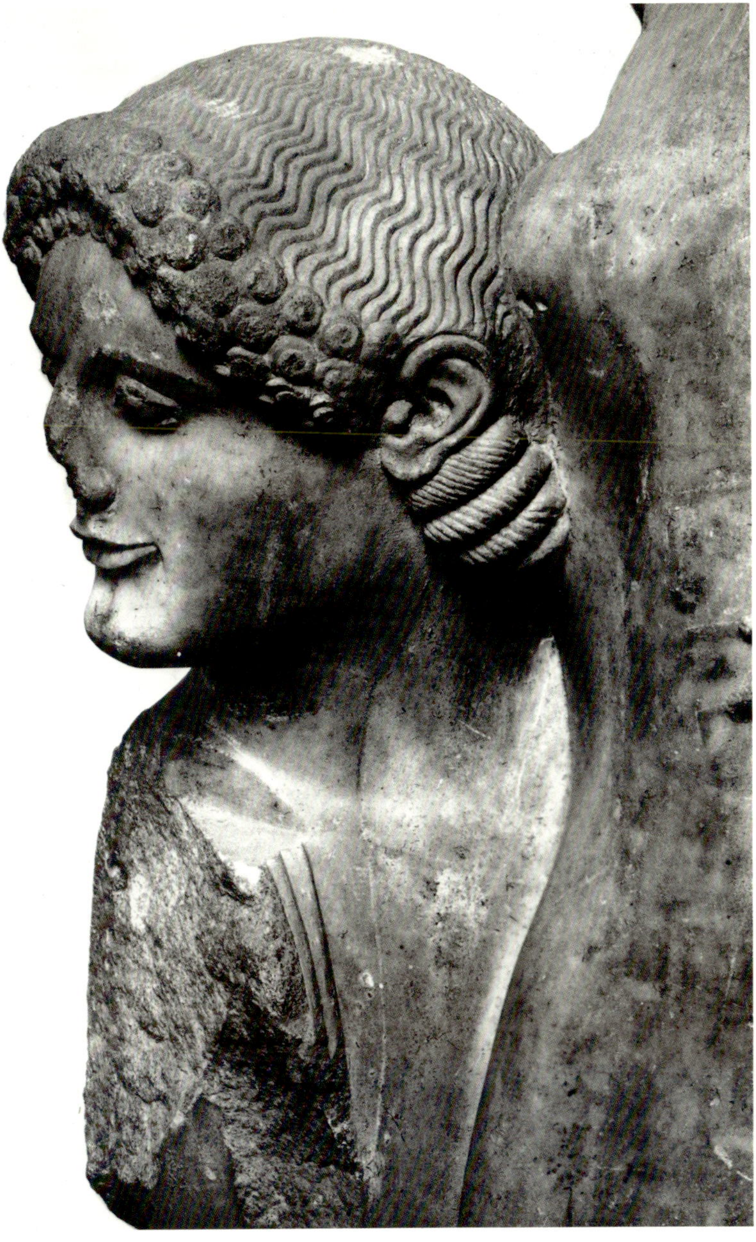

53. **Head of Theseus** from the pediment (see fig. 56).

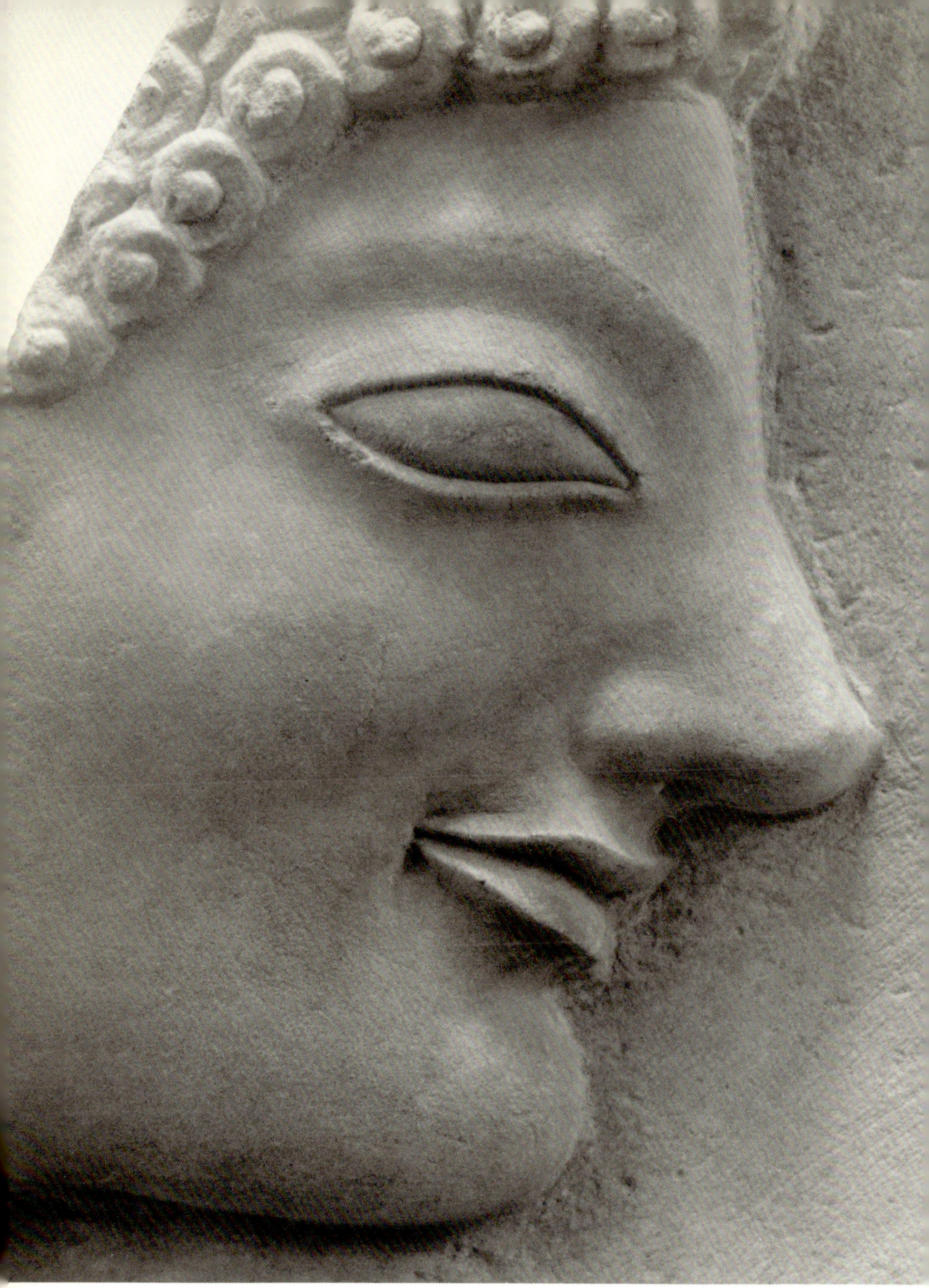

54. Head of the younger man from the Getty relief.

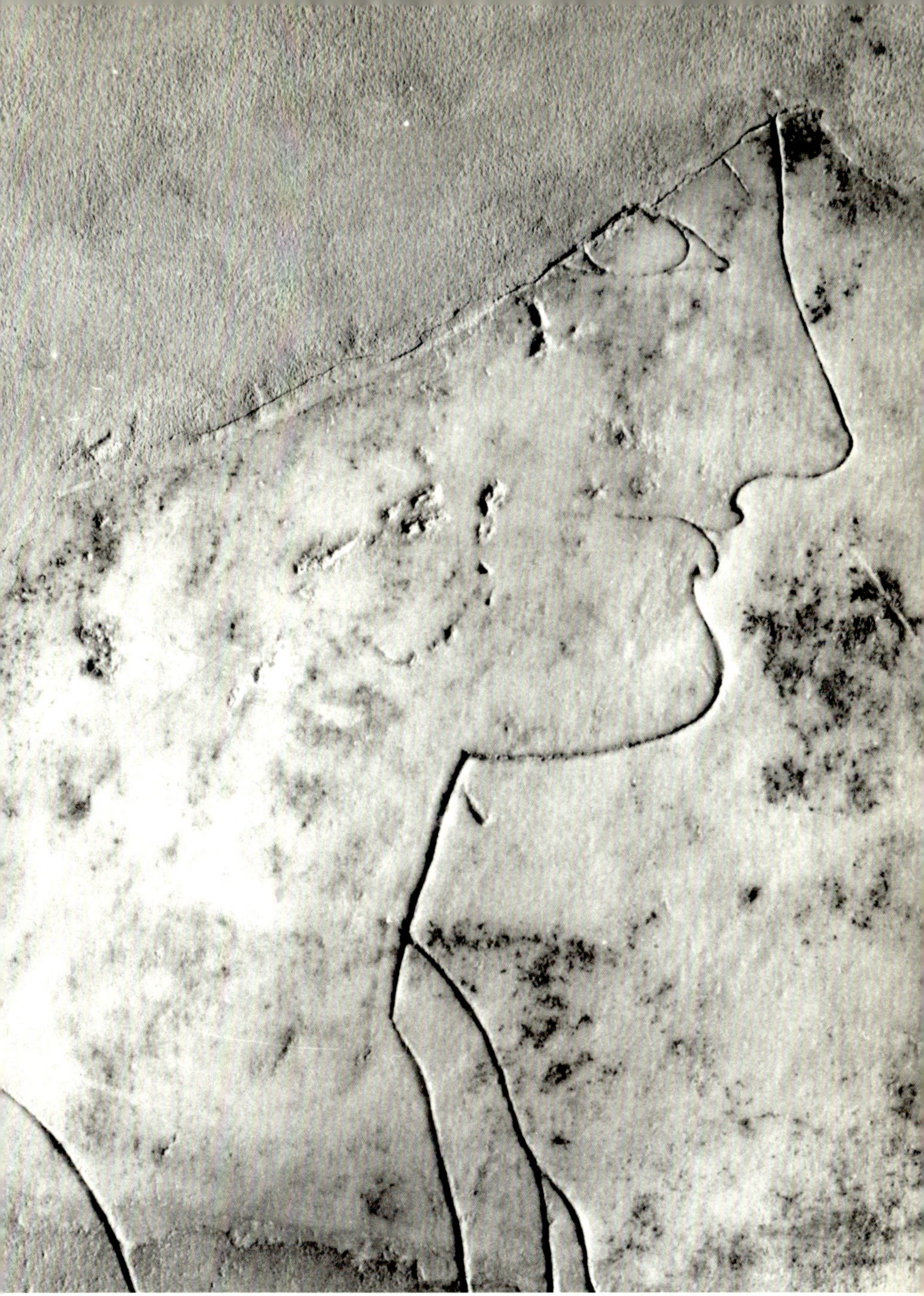

55. **Head of the youth** from the engraved stele (detail of fig. 41).

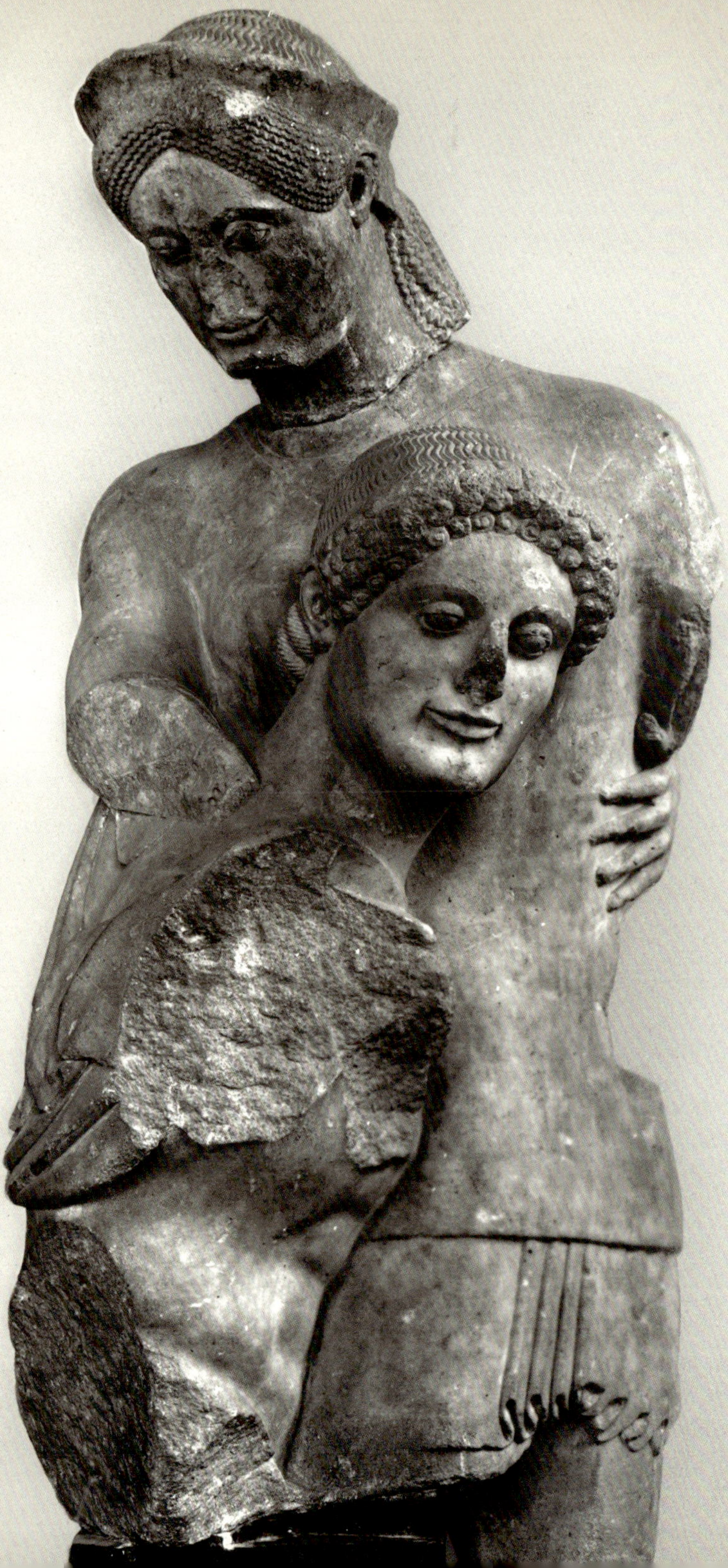

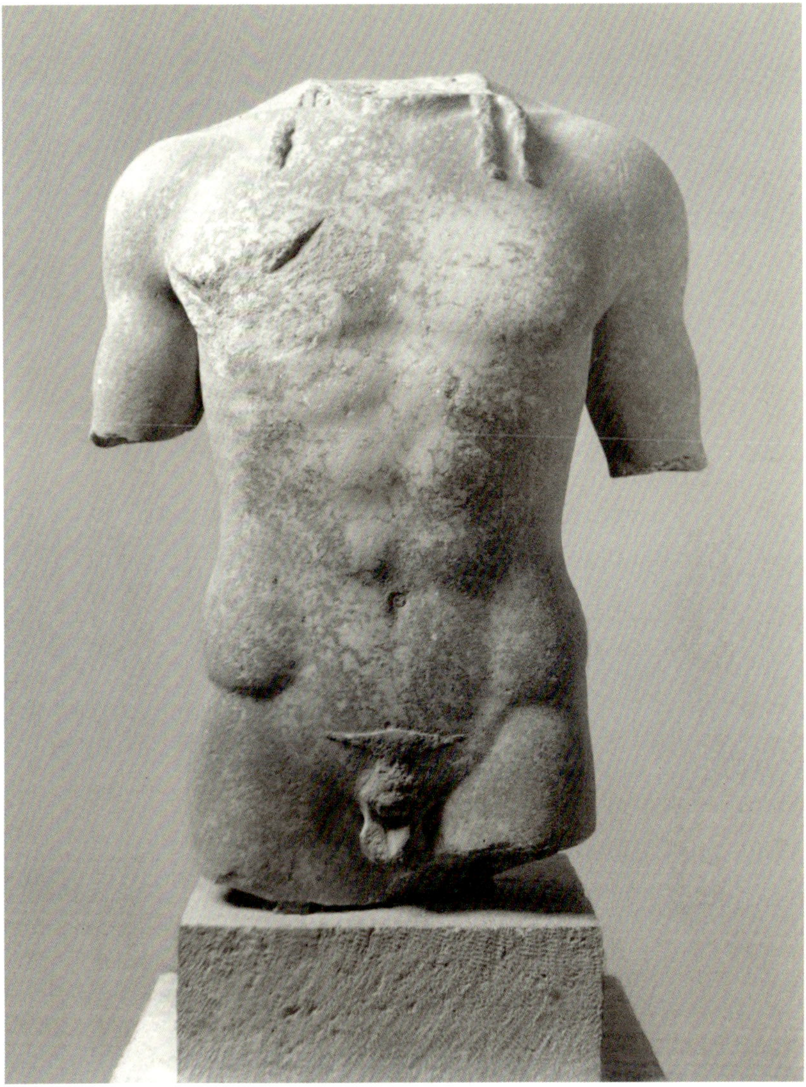

57. Torso of a kouros. 500–490 B.C. By the same hand as the Getty relief. Chalkis, Museum.

56. Group of Theseus and Antiope from the west pediment of the temple of Apollo Daphnephoros in Eretria (Euboia). 510–500 B.C. By the same hand as the Getty relief. Chalkis, Museum.

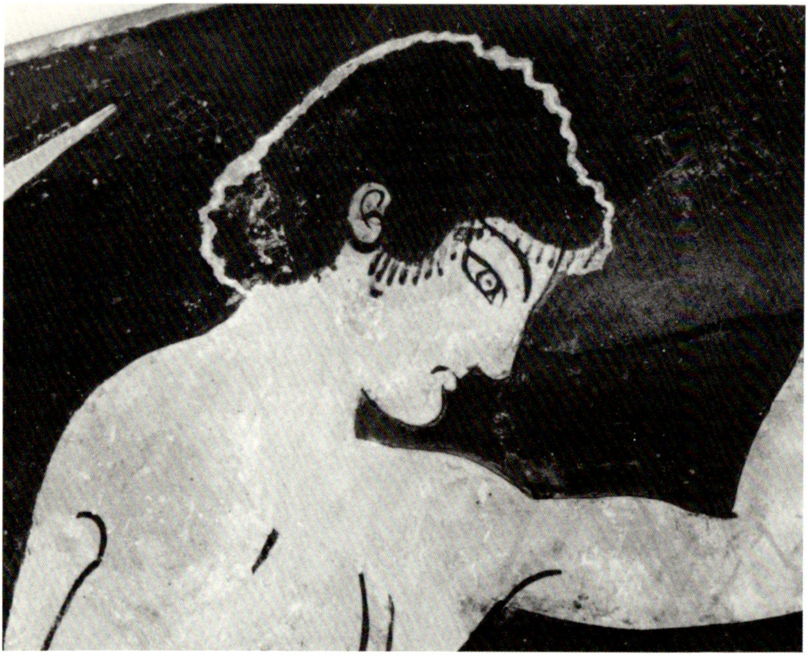

58. Detail from an Attic red-figure cup signed by the vase painter Phintias; profile of Phintias himself. Ca. 510 B.C. The same clean profile, rounded chin, and softly modeled hair appear as on the Chalkis and Getty sculptures. Malibu, The J. Paul Getty Museum.

Peplos Kore.[104] His figures share the Peplos Kore's solid build, but their spirit is totally different—they really do smile. He was able to assimilate, perhaps better than any of his compatriots, the lessons of the sculptors of East Greece, who were fleeing to Athens from the Persian invasion during his time. Against the secure background of the traditional Attic *gravitas,* he evokes the enchantment of the art emanating from the lifestyle of the rich, pleasure-loving, and carefree Greeks from Asia Minor. Avoiding the purely decorative trend of East Greek art, he was always ready to adopt many details from his Attic contemporaries. For example, the undercut zigzag folds on the group from Eretria (fig. 56) are an adaptation of a motif current in the work of Antenor, a staunch Athenian. The zigzag appears not only on Antenor's signed Kore (fig. 59)[105] but also on the figures from the east pediment of Apollo's temple in Delphi,[106] predating the Eretria pediment.

The sculptor's ties with Euboia may have been yet stronger. Two

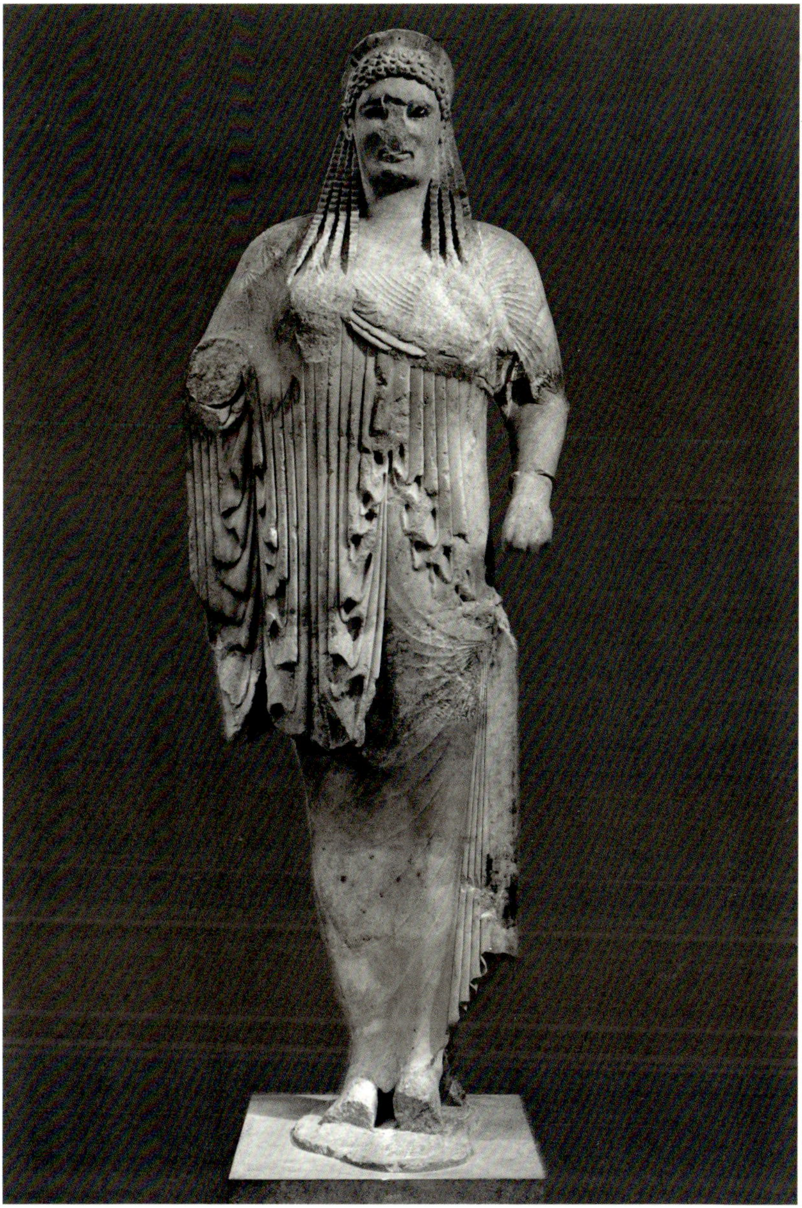

59. A girl dedicated on the Athenian Acropolis by Nearchos the potter and signed by the sculptor Antenor. After 520 B.C. Athens, Acropolis Museum.

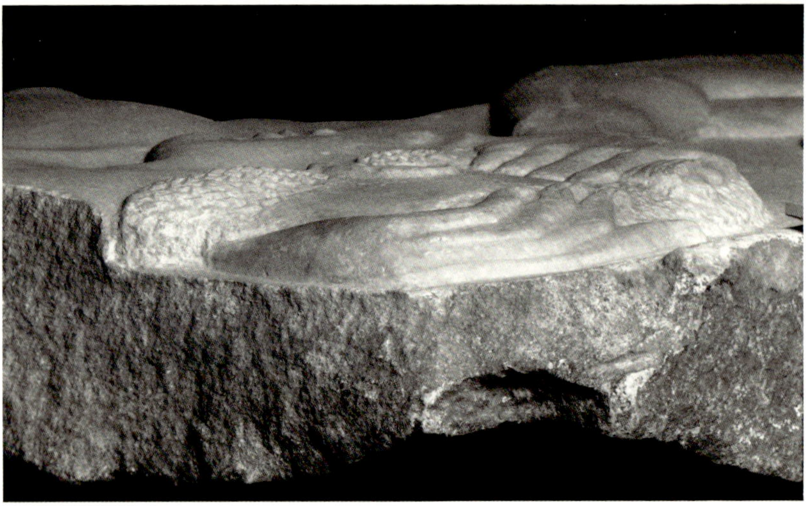

60. **The Getty relief.** Detail of the head of the dying man from the side.

heads of kouroi found in Eretria, one dating about the mid-sixth century,[107] the other soon after,[108] look like ancestors of the Theseus from the pediment. All three men have heavy, low jaws; the relation of the orbits and facial bones is also identical. The heads of the two kouroi appear considerably inferior, but this is due to some extent to their poor preservation. The style can be taken for Attic but displays an unmistakable local color. The inevitable conclusion is that the master of the Getty relief began his career as an apprentice in a workshop on this island. Later, when he was already a mature artist, his countrymen commissioned the pedimental sculptures for the major temple of Eretria from him.

There are some other particular features in the master's work. He was clearly an expert in painting as well as in sculpture. Of course his marbles were probably painted by himself. Clear traces of paint survive on the stele of mother with child (fig. 6): the drapery between the two figures was only painted with an ornamental edge, but behind the child's head is a fold raised in sculptural relief. The Louvre stele (fig. 41) was mainly a pictorial work, contrasting large areas of lively colors rather than relying on linear drawing. A strong pictorial element

61. **The Getty relief** from an angle, emphasizing the three-dimensionality of its concept.

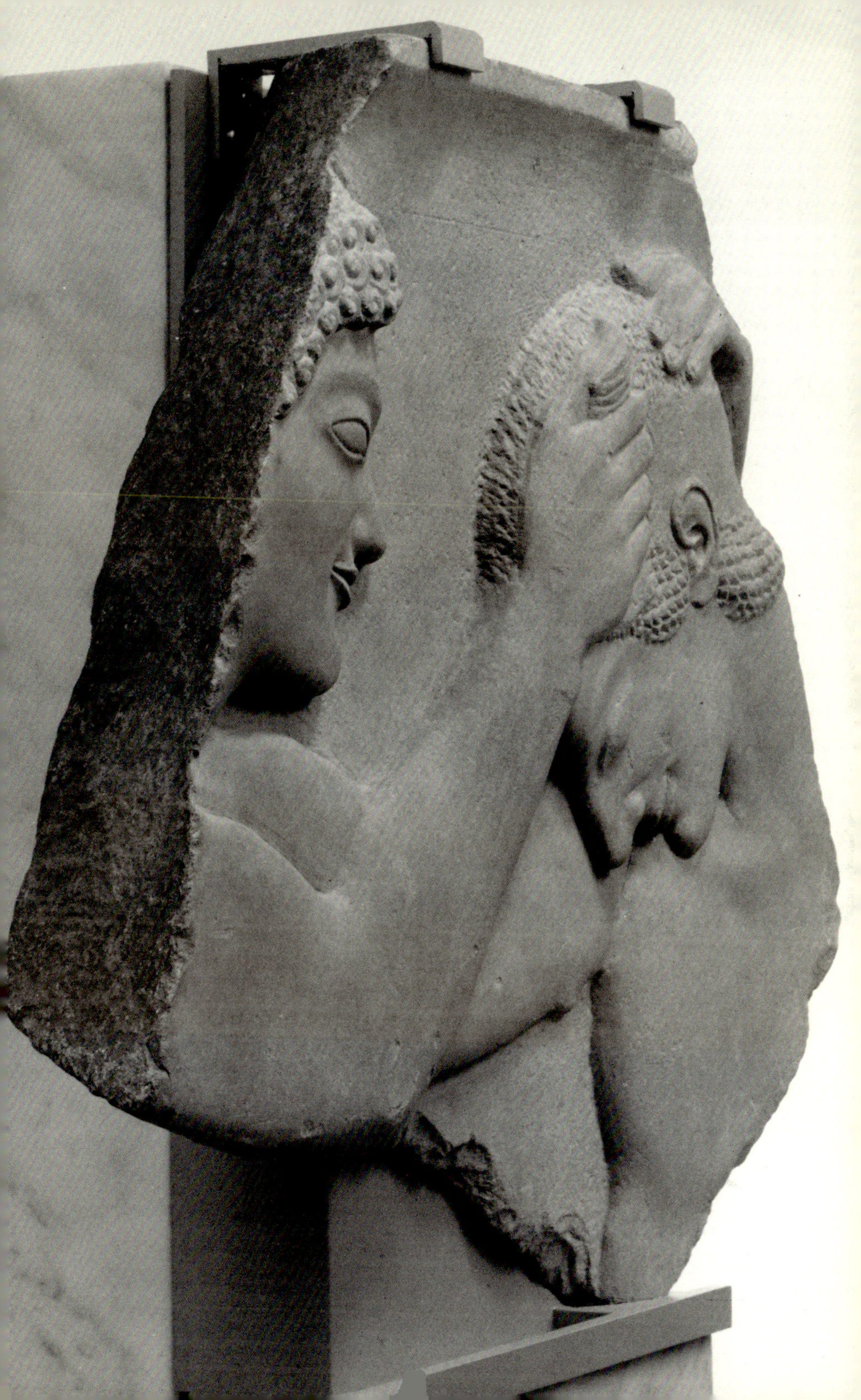

also appears in the other reliefs, and not only because originally they were made more lively by the application of much polychromy and gilt. The sculptor's known compositions, from the frieze of the Kerameikos Museum base (fig. 47), as reflected in the later replica by another sculptor (fig. 48), to both the mother with child and Getty relief stelai are treated as much as painted panels as sculptural groups. Even the three-dimensional statuary of the Eretria pediment (fig. 56) uses illusionistic effects adopted from painting. What survives does not give a clear indication of the group, but it is evident that Theseus was lifting the abducted Antiope into a chariot around which the other figures must have been arranged. The artist courageously attacked the spatial limitations of the shallow triangular pediment, achieving an unusual illusion of depth in his composition.

Another important characteristic of the sculptor concerns the technical procedures he uses. They are found in their fullest form in the Eretria pediment, and from them one can understand some of the peculiarities of the Getty relief. First, the sculptor is extremely efficient at utilizing even the smallest scraps of marble. Only the workshop that a decade later (after 490 B.C.) carved the sculptural decoration of the Athenian treasury at Delphi was comparably inventive in saving the precious and difficult to transport material. The bows of the Amazons in the Eretria pediment are pieced together with metal joins, as are the legs of the horses and the limbs of the other humans. Sometimes even a little missing body part is carefully fitted in place. Also of interest is the mixture of relief and three-dimensional carving for the pedimental sculptures. Some of the horse legs and the thigh of Theseus have only the front half carved in the round, while the back is a flat surface intended to adhere to the back wall of the pediment. All the large sculptures, not only the central figure of Athena or the horses but even the group of Theseus and Antiope, do not support themselves on their feet but were instead attached to the background of the pediment. A large rectangular cavity in each figure was filled with a marble prism that was put in a corresponding cavity in the back wall of the pediment and fixed in place with lead. From the surviving remnants, it is clear that this final stage of attachment was carried out not by the master sculptor but by technicians who were skilled in the use of lead but who were not particularly careful of the back parts of the marble sculptures. There is a similar small rectangular pentimento of repair on the right collarbone of the kouros. The small cavities on the top of the relief and its picked reverse are easier to understand in this connection.

Perhaps the most unusual feature of this archaic sculptor is his capacity for expressing emotions. While the action in the ball game corresponds to standard depictions of athletic scenes, the tender care of the mother for her child and the friendship of the two companions on the Getty relief are unique and special. No less impressive is the lyrical treatment of the abduction of the consenting Antiope and the sensuality of the Chalkis torso. Lacking the effeminacy of the so-called "beautiful" torso from the Acropolis,[109] the kouros is the last blossom of the archaic, to be superseded by the rectangular severity of the Kritios boy.[110]

This proposed oeuvre places the artist among the greatest Athenian masters, among the greatest creators of archaic Greek art. Like the poet Anakreon, the sculptor of the Getty relief worked for the rich patrons of his time. The Anavysos and Euboia sites point to the gentry of the Attic countryside and its immediate neighborhood. The poet Simonides, another professional, also divided his time between Athens and Euboia during the same years.

Three stages may be distinguished in the work of our master. The stele of the mother with the child and the base with the ball players belong to his early years. The Getty relief and the stele in the Louvre show the ripening sculptor. The pediment and the torso of the kouros were carved at full maturity of his art. The turning point from his prime is clearly marked by a change of two essential elements. The virtuoso modeling becomes so sophisticated that the surface of the marble appears to vibrate; the breath of the creator has awakened the soul of the transparent *lychnites,* the best Parian marble. But still more striking is the smile; omnipresent in archaic sculpture, it reaches in the Getty relief, in the Louvre stele, and in the Eretria pediments a radiant intensity hardly surpassed in the realm of antiquity. The Golden Age of Italy coined a similar approach to the smile as a mirror of human emotions. For Dante, the presence of Beatrice was inseparable from the vision of her smiling lips inviting a kiss. And the same smile appears in the Florentine painting of the High Renaissance. The Mona Lisa comes to mind first, but the closest kin of the youths on the Getty relief may be some smiling faces on other drawings of Leonardo da Vinci (fig. 63). *ποντίων τε κυμάτων ἀνήριθμον γέλασμα*: "the unaccountable smile of the sea's waves..."[111] keeps its pulse alive above the merciless flow of Lethe.

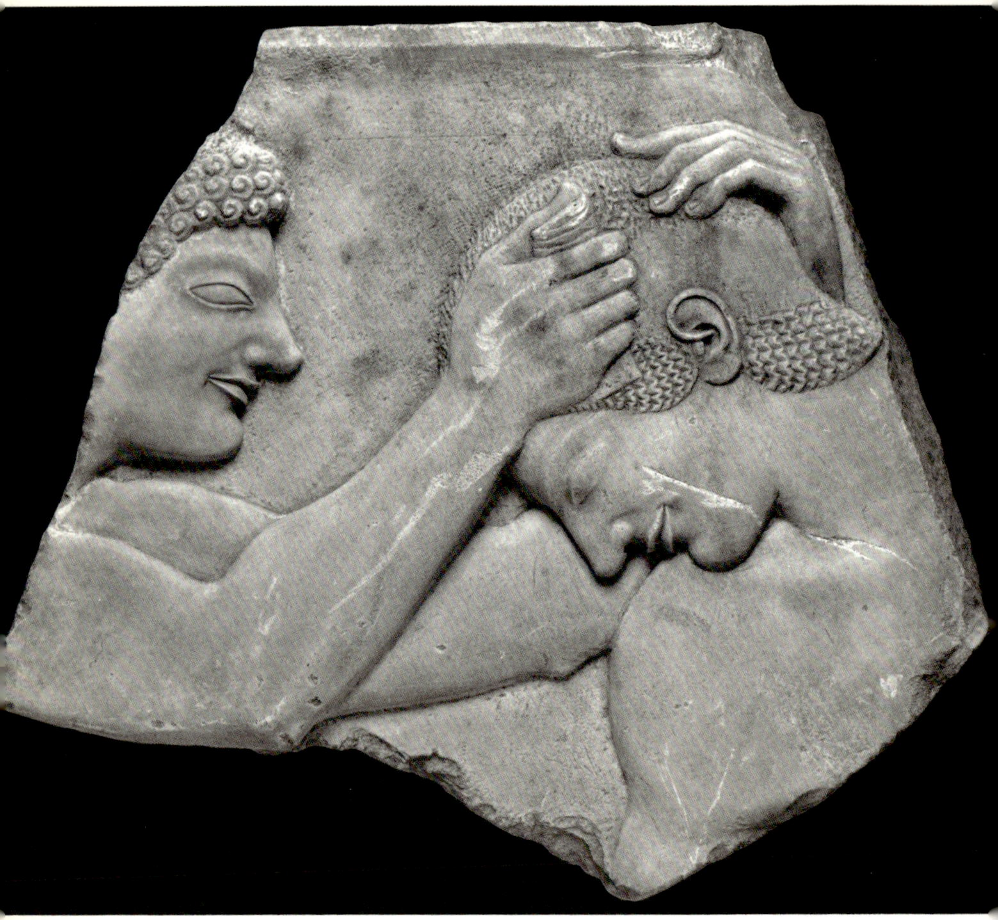

62. **The Getty relief** before conservation.

63. **Leonardo da Vinci**, detail of the face of the Virgin from the cartoon of the *Virgin and Child with St. Anne and the Infant St. John* in charcoal on brown paper. London, the National Gallery.

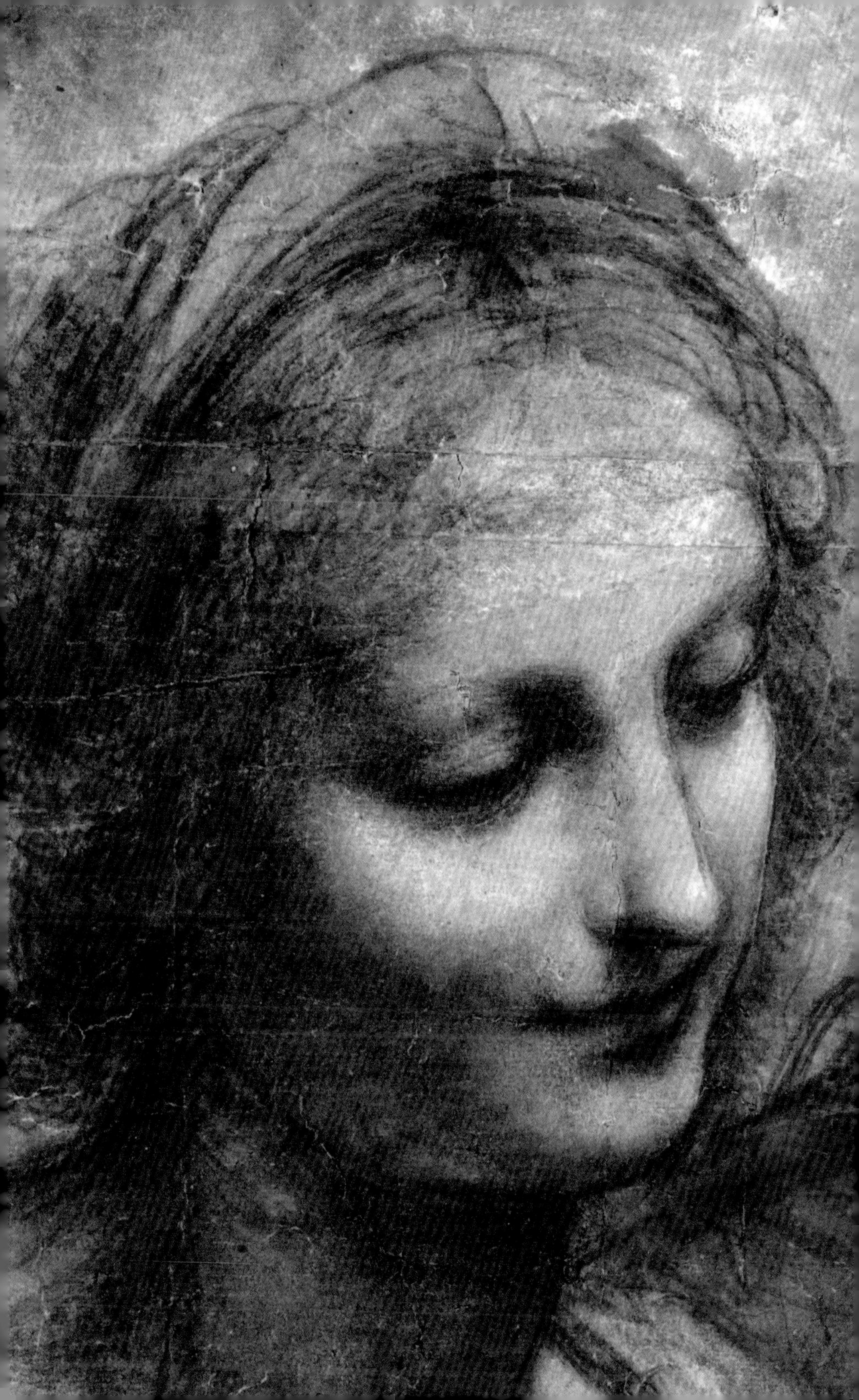

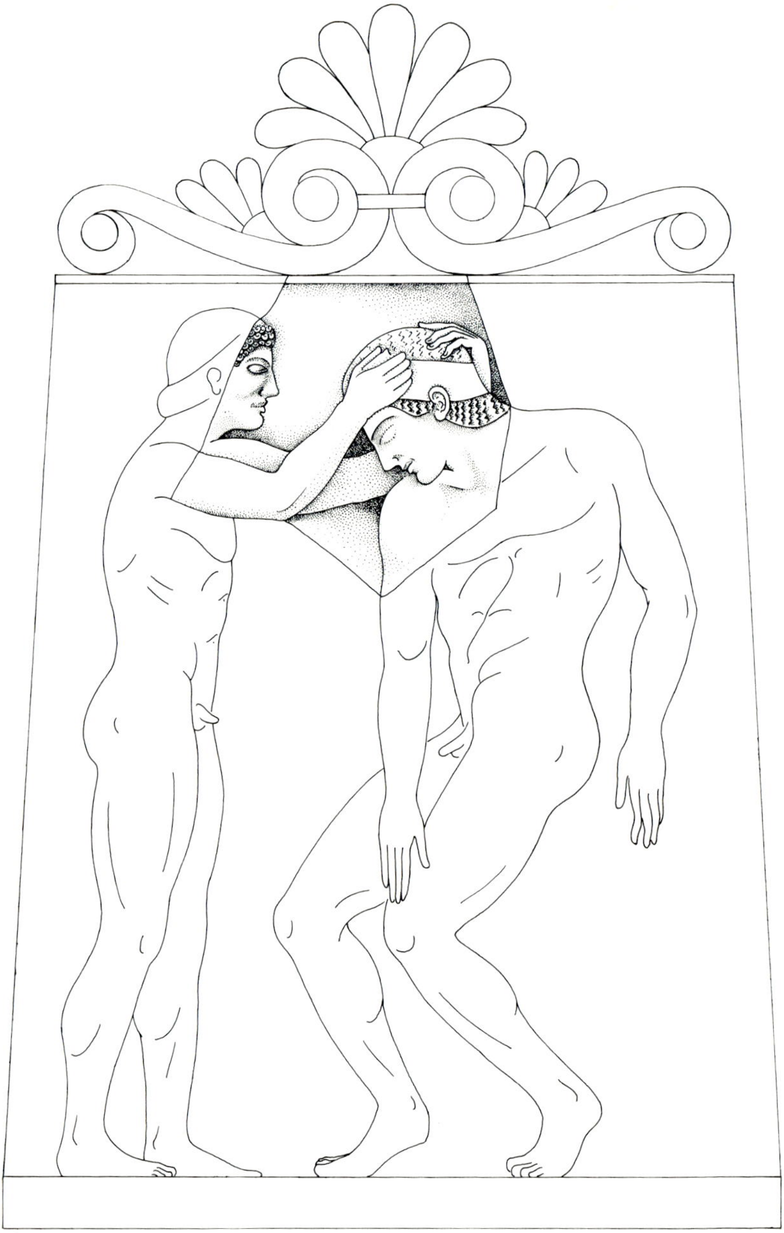

64. Reconstruction of the original appearance of the Getty relief. Drawing by Martha Breen Bredemeyer after the author.

Notes

This text was presented to the public at the J. Paul Getty Museum (1980 and 1982), at the University of California at Santa Barbara (1981), and in two lectures at the Collège de France (April 1982). My thanks are due to the conservation, photo, and publication departments. The manuscript was read and improved by Faya Causey Frel, Arthur Houghton, Marion True, Sheldon Nodelman, J. Gy. Szilagyi, Dietrich Willers, and Sandra Knudsen Morgan.

Two Friends

1. The J. Paul Getty Museum, 79.AA.1.
Finest Parian marble, height: 49 cm, width: 59 cm, depth of the slab: 6.9 cm, depth including the relief: 9-9.3 cm, at the top 8.9 cm. The top edge protrudes forming a molding 1.1 cm high. On each side of the top is a small cavity, the right better preserved, 4.5 cm x more than 2.7 cm x 1.6 cm, for the metallic pins holding the lost finial. 5.9 cm below, an incised guideline gives the lower limit of the vanished painted pattern. Cleaned by Z. Barov in 1979; small damaged areas above the right head, on its cheek, next to the corner of the mouth, and on the neck. Some minor scratches painted over.
Bibliography: J. Frel, "Notes on Some Archaic Attic Sculpture," Getty *MJ* 10 (1982) no. 11, 98–104; C. C. Vermeule, *Greek and Roman Sculpture in America* (Berkeley, 1982) no. 5; J. Frel, *The J. Paul Getty Museum, Catalogue of The Collections. Antiquities. Greek Originals* 1 (in preparation), no. 3.

2. Oral communication of E. Langlotz in 1973; he saw the monument in 1931 on the art market.

3. 1. The kouros from Anavysos, Athens, National Museum 3851. Richter, *Kouroi,* 118sqq., no. 136, *figs. 395–398,* 400; Deyhle 1969, pl. 3.2; E. Mastrokostas, "Die drei Stufen des Kroisos-Kuros," *AAA* 7 (1974) 215sqq. (base); Frel 1982, 95.
2. Grave relief of mother and child, Athens, National Museum 4472. Richter, *Gravestones,* no. 53, *figs. 151–153;* Frel 1982, 99.1, *fig. 3* (detail).
3. Engraved grave relief of a youth, Louvre Ma 3432. Richter, *Gravestones,* no. 57, *figs. 138–139;* Frel 1982, 99, 101 *fig. 5* (detail).
Nos. 2 and 3 are by the same sculptor as our relief, see above pp. 51–52.

What is Represented

4. Berlin F2278, by the Sosias Painter. *ARV*² 21.1,1620; *CVA* pls. 49–50.* See also *Ancient Greek Art and Iconography,* ed. Warren G. Moon (Madison, 1983) 144, notes 76 and 78.

5. Louvre CA 2183. *ARV*² 803, 813sq., 96; *Para.* 420.

6. *Supra* n. 3, no 2.

7. M. Napoli, *Paestum* (Novara, 1973) *fig. 92;* N. Daniele, *Paestum* (Berlin, 1979) *figs. 76, 77;* Boardman-La Rocca 1975, 104–105.

8. *ARV*² 367.93; Boardman-La Rocca 1975, 114.

9. There are countless examples of the subject, cf. for example a cup by Onesimos in the Bareiss collection: *Para.* 360 92ter, or the well-known cup by the Brygos Painter in Würzburg: *ARV*² 372.32.

10. *Supra* n. 3, no. 2.

11. New York, The Metropolitan Museum of Art 1972.11.10. D. von Bothmer, "Greek

Vase Painting: An Introduction," *BulMetMus* 31 (1972) 2sqq.; idem, "Der Euphronioskrater in New York," *AA* (1976) 485sqq.; J. Boardman, *Athenian Red Figure Vases. The Archaic Period* (London, 1975) frontispiece and *fig. 22.*

12. Calyx krater: Malibu, The J. Paul Getty Museum 77.AE.5 and 82.AE.24. M. Robertson, "The Berlin Painter at the Getty Museum and Some Others," *GrVases* 1. *OPA* 1 (1983) 55sqq. (only the fragments available in 1980 are reproduced). The comparison of the Achilles' head with that of Sarpedon on the New York Krater (see n. 11) shows how much the Berlin Painter owes to Euphronios.

13. J. P. Vernant, "La belle mort et le cadavre outragé," *Journal de psychologie,* nos. 2–3 (1980) 209–241. See also E. T. Vermeule, *Aspects of Death in Early Greek Art and Poetry* (Berkeley, 1979).

Kalos Thanatos

14. *Iliad* xxii 52sqq.

15. The best version of Perikles' speech is recorded by the historian Thucydides ii 35sqq., but the quotation here is from a similar context (funeral oration over the Athenians fallen in the Samian revolt) as reported in Plutarch's *Perikles* vii. 6.

16. Herodotos i 30; our text is a free translation.

Men Among Men

17. Thucydides ii 46.

18. Copenhagen, Ny Carlsberg Glyptotek I.N.2787. Richter, *Gravestones,* no. 77, *fig. 172.*

19. The best summary is still E. Langlotz, *Zur Zeitbestimmung der strengrotfigurigen Vasenmalerei und der gleichzeitigen Plastik* (Leipzig, 1920) 43sqq.

20. *Ibid.,* 48sqq.; *ABV* 669; *ARV*[2] 507sqq., 1699; *Para.* 507; cf. also Francis-Vickers 1981, 97sqq.; G. Zimmer, "Der Schmied in der Schale," *JbBerlMus* 24 (1982) 12sq.

21. Herodotos ix 75.

22. *ARV*[2] 1580sq.; *Para.* 506.

23. Cf. Francis-Vickers 1981, 99, n. 39.

24. *Iliad* xviii 98sq.

25. See S. Brunnsaker, *The Tyrantslayers of Kritios and Nesiotes* (Stockholm, second ed., 1971).

26. B. D. Meritt, *Inscriptions from the Athenian Agora* (Picturebook no. 10, 1966) no. 4. A marble splinter with some words of this inscription was recovered in the American excavation of the Athenian Agora; another bit is preserved in a treatise on Greek metric written in Roman times as an example of how to press an odd word into prosody: the name Aristogeiton is split into two verses.

27. Malibu, The J. Paul Getty Museum, 74.AA.12. O. M. von Stackelberg, *Die Gräber der Hellenen* (Berlin, 1837) 33; J. Frel, "Some Notes on the Elgin Throne," *AM* 91 (1976) 185sqq. (bibl.); L. Beschi, "L.S. Fauvel e il c.d. Trono Elgin," Getty *MJ* 5 (1977) 33sqq.

28. Getty 83.AE.322 and Louvre G 25 (*ARV*[2] 316.5, 1592.14) with vomiting Leagros.

The Fashion of Hair

29. Chalkis, Museum. R. Lullies-M. Hirmer, *Greek Sculpture* (New York, 1957) pls. 62–64; Bothmer 1957, 124sq., pl. 471; Frel 1982, 99, no. 4, 101, *fig. 6,* 103, *8* (details).

30. B. Schlörb-Vierneisel, "Zwei klassische Kindergräber im Kerameikos," *AM* 79 (1964) 93sqq., Beil. 48.1sqq.; J. Frel, "The Krito Sculptor," *AAA* 3 (1970) 370sq.; Kurtz-Boardman 1971, *fig. 30.*

31. Malibu, The J. Paul Getty Museum 68.AA.21 and 22, 71.AA.461. All three appear in

C. Vermeule-N. Neuerburg, *Catalogue of the Ancient Art in The J. Paul Getty Museum* (Malibu, 1973) nos. 39–41. Also, "Polyhymnia" L. 73.AA.24, lent by Hans Cohn, illustrated in the 1981 J. Paul Getty Museum Appointment Calendar, December 28.

32. *Iliad* xvii 51sq.

33. Paris, Louvre G 103. *ARV*² 14.2. The original foot was identified by A. Pasquier, "Nouvelles découvertes à propos du cratère d'Antée peint par Euphronios," *La Revue du Louvre* 31 (1981) lsqq.

34. Bilingual neck amphora of special sub-Nikosthenic shape (the Adikia Subclass). Vienna, Kunsthistorisches Museum 3722: *ABV* 320.11; *ARV*² 11.3, 1618; *Para.* 139.1.

35. Red figure skyphos by the Brygos Painter. Boston, Museum of Fine Arts 10.176: *ARV*² 381.173.

36. Herodotos vii 208–209.

Greek Funerary Monuments

37. Johansen 1951, 68sq.; Richter, *Gravestones,* Kurtz-Boardman 1971, 21sqq., 31sq., 49sq., 56sqq.

38. K. Kübler, "Ausgrabungen im Kerameikos," *AA* (1936) 185sq.; Richter, *Gravestones, fig. 27.*

39. A. Bruckner, *Der Friedhof am Eridanos* (Berlin, 1909); G. Karo, *An Attic Cemetery* (Philadelphia, 1943).

40. Kurtz-Boardman 1971, 90.

41. *Ibid.,* 88sq.: Richter, *Kouroi,* no. 6, *figs. 50–53, 63–67* (+ 7 *54–59, 68*); 11, *76–77;* 134, *388–390;* 136, *395–398, 400;* 161bis, *483–484;* 165, *489, 492–493.*

42. Kurtz-Boardman 1971, *1.1;* Richter, *Korai,* no. 42, *figs. 139–146;* 91, *284–285;* Richter, *Gravestones,* 24sq., 157, *figs. 94, 200;* N. Kontoleon, *Aspects de la Grèce préclassique* (Paris, 1970) 53sqq., 59sqq., 89sqq. *figs. 3–4,* pl. XV; and E. Mastrokostas, "e kore Phrasikleia Aristionos tou Pariou kai kouros marmarinos anekalyphthesan en Myrrinounti," *AAA* 5 (1972) 298sqq.

43. Richter, *Kouroi, figs. 9–11; 12–13;* no. 159bis, *478–480;* 181, *533–540.*

44. Richter, *Kouroi;* Delphi: *figs. 14–16,* no. 42, *157–159;* 103, *339;* 104, *340;* 105, *335;* 106, *330–333;* 149, *440;* 150, *438–439;* many others can be traced. Delos: *20–21; 22–24;* 15, *87–90;* 17, *94–95;* 48, *176–177;* 110, *341, 344;* 111, *342, 345;* 112, *343, 346;* 130; 151, *443–444;* 152, *445–446;* 174, *521, 524;* Naxos: 175, *515–517.* Samos: 77, *258–60.* Ptoion: cf. J. Ducat, *Les kouroi de Ptoion* (Paris, 1971) 103sqq. (This essential publication was inaccessible when preparing the article, Frel 1982, 95sqq.)

45. C. Karouzos, *Aristodikos* (Stuttgart, 1961), appendix; only for grave stelai: Richter, *Gravestones.* 155 (M. Guarducci); L. Jeffery, "The Inscribed Gravestones of Archaic Attica," *BSA* 57 (1962) 115sqq.

46. Cf. *supra* n. 3, no. 1.

47. For the inscription, see Richter, *Kouroi,* p. 115 and *fig. 401.*

48. Richter, *Gravestones,* no. 20, *figs. 66–69;* 23, *86;* 46, *129;* 48, *130;* 64, *154, 178;* 65, *162;* 66, *165;* 68, *161;* 77, *172* and notes 18, 49, 50 below; Schmalz 1983, 167.

49. Athens, National Museum 29. *Ibid.,* no. 67, *figs. 155–157,* 180; the kneecaps were recarved in antiquity.

50. New York, The Metropolitan Museum of Art 36.11.13. *Ibid.,* no. 45, *figs. 126–128. 179* (the sphinx: *ibid.,* 38, *110–114,* belongs to the same funerary stele); for the polychromy, cf. Richter 1944, 324sqq., 335, pl. IX (L. Hall); another case of a well-preserved and documented polychromy is the limestone sphinx i New York, The Metropolitan Museum of Art: Richter, *Gravestones,* 14, 4649; Richter 1944, 324, 335, pl. X.

51. *Supra* n. 18.

52. Richter, *Gravestones,* no. 26, *fig. 88;* 28, *80–82;* 31, *92,* a new stele in the National Museum of Athens, found in the Themistoclean wall, with a youth with an aryballos M 1572, BE 9/74 and notes 50, 51, and 52. Schmalz 1983, 168.

53. There is a new, unpublished stele in the National Museum of Athens, found in the Themistoclean wall, representing a youth with a crown M 1541, BE 8/74.

54. Malibu, The J. Paul Getty Museum 82.AA.54, anonymous donation; ex-collection R. Schmidt, Solothurn; Pentelic marble, preserved height: 21.5 cm. Richter, *Gravestones,* no. 32, *fig. 91.*

55. Athens, National Museum 38. Richter, *Gravestones,* no. 25, *fig. 77;* another fragment *ibid.,* preserves one leg, to which the other, recently found, was added, cf. F. Willemsen, "Stelen. Grab- und Weihinschriften," *AM* 85 (1970) 28sq., pl. 11.3.

56. New York, The Metropolitan Museum 11.185. Berlin, Staatliche Museen A7. Richter, *Gravestones,* no. 37, *figs. 96–109, 190;* idem, *Korai,* 137, *439–440;* idem, "The Story of the 'Megakles' Stele in New York," *Mélanges Mansel* (1974) 1sqq., pls. 1sqq.

57. For example, the diskophoros stele (*supra* n. 51) or a glorious fragment in New York, The Metropolitan Museum of Art, Richter, *Gravestones,* no. 52, *fig. 132,* to which *ibid.* 43, *125* belongs. Not near Peplos Kore, pace Ch. C. Tsirivaku, Z. Neumann, "Zum Meister der Peploskore," *AM* 79 (1964) 114sqq.

Funerary Stelai

58. Richter, *Gravestones,* 4sqq.; Schmalz 1983, 59sqq.

59. Richter, *Gravestones,* 9, *figs. 27, 28.*

60. *Ibid.,* 10sqq.

61. *Ibid.,* 6.

62. *Ibid.,* 2sqq.

63. *Ibid.,* 53.

64. Athens, National Museum 737. Johansen 1951, 48sqq.; Schmalz 1983, XVI sq. (bibl.), 189sqq. (general evolution).

65. Malibu, The J. Paul Getty Museum 77.AA.89. Cf. Johansen 1951, 13sqq., 53sqq.

66. Kurtz-Boardman 1971, 166.

67. Cicero, *De legibus* ii 26.44.

68. The available evidence in favor of 317 may be confused, cf. Kurtz-Boardman 1971, 162.

69. Malibu, The J. Paul Getty Museum 71.AA.288. Schmalz 1983, 223sqq.

70. Malibu, The J. Paul Getty Museum 73.AA.114.

71. Athens, National Museum 1959. M. Andronikos, "Peri tis stilis tou Hoplitoudromou," *Eph* 1953/54 (1958) 317sqq. As funerary, for example: G. Lippold, *Die Griechische Plastik* (Munich, 1950) 84; as votive: Richter, *Gravestones* 42, n. 11; Johansen 1951, 103, n. 1.

72. *Supra* n. 3, no. 2.

Carving a Stele

73. The best survey of the subject remains C. Blümel, *Greek Sculptors at Work* (London, second ed., 1969).

74. Richter, *Gravestones,* 4sqq.

75. Reutersward 1960, *passim;* Richter, *Gravestones,* 6; Schmalz 1983, XIXsq. (bibl.), 71sqq.

76. *Supra* n. 50.

77. Athens, National Museum 30; Richter, *Gravestones,* no. 70. Louvre Ma 3432; *supra* n. 3, no. 3.

78. Reuterswärd 1960, 44.

Sculptor of the Getty Relief

79. *Supra* n. 3, no. 2.

80. *ABV* 145.14.

81. Athens, Acropolis Museum 673, Payne 1954, 35sq., pls. 62–64; Richter, *Korai,* no. 117, *figs. 368–372;* Brouskari 1974, 63sq., *figs. 114–115.*

82. Athens, Acropolis Museum 670. Payne 1954, 37sqq., pls. 65–67; Richter, *Korai,* no. 119, *figs. 377–380;* Brouskari 1974, 70sq., *figs. 131–132.*

83. Athens, Acropolis Museum 679. Payne 1954, 18sq., 29sqq., pls. 29–33; Richter, *Korai,* no. 113, *figs. 349–354;* Brouskari 1974, 56sq., *figs. 100–101.*

84. Athens, Acropolis Museum 643. Payne 1954, 66sq. pls. 70–71; Richter, *Korai,* no. 128, *figs. 417–419;* Brouskari 1974, 66sq., *fig. 122.* For the attributions, cf. Frel 1982, 96.

85. Athens, National Museum 3476. J. Boardman, *Greek Sculpture: The Archaic Period,* (London, 1980) 292; Frel 1982, 99.

86. F. Willemsen, "Archäische Grabmalbasen aus der Athener Stadmauer," *AM* 78 (1963) pls. 64.2, 65.1–2, 66.1.

87. Frel 1982, 98sq.

88. Cf. *ibid.*

89. *Supra* n. 3, no. 2.

90. Deyhle 1969, 28.

91. See n. 29.

92. Richter, *Kouroi,* no. 168, *figs. 494–496.*

93. See n. 77.

94. Cf. the drawings of the Andokides Painter, *ARV*² 35sq.

95. For the chronology of the Andokides Painter, see D. von Bothmer, *BMMA* (February 1966) 201–212.

96. *ARV*² 54.9sqq., 58.51sqq.

97. Cf. J. Charbonneaux, "Stèle archaique gravée du Musée du Louvre," *MonPiot* 37 (1940) 46sqq.

98. Malibu, The J. Paul Getty Museum 80.AE.31. *ARV*² 1620, as 12bis on p. 74.

99. See n. 29.

100. Cf. especially the solid, round heads of the arming youths on the reverse. For the vase, see n. 11.

101. Richter, *Kouroi,* no. 161, *figs. 481–482;* 161bis, *483–484;* 165, *489, 492–493.*

102. Touloupa 1983, Kat. I 55, pl. 38.2.

103. Cf. e.g. representations by the Andokides Painter, *ARV* 3.1, 2.

104. Cf. the summary in Frel 1982, 96.

105. Payne 1954, 31sq., 63sq., pls. 51–53, 124.5; Richter, *Korai,* no. 110, *figs. 336–340;* Brouskari 1974, 78sqq., *figs. 152–153.*

106. Richter, *Korai,* no. 106, *figs. 324–326;* 107, *322–323.*

107. Richter, *Kouroi,* no. 102, *figs. 325, 329.*

108. *Ibid.,* no. 168, *figs. 494–496.*

109. Payne 1954, 46, pl. 108; Richter, *Kouroi,* no. 160, *figs. 464–466;* Brouskari 1974, 131, *fig. 250.*

110. Payne 1954, 44, pls. 109–112; Richter, *Kouroi,* no. 190, *figs. 564–569;* Brouskari 1974, 124, *fig. 238.*

111. Aischylos, *Prometheus* 89sq.

Abbreviations

J. Boardman and E. La Rocca 1975. *Eros in Grecia.* Milan.

D. von Bothmer 1957. *Amazons in Greek Art.* Oxford.

M. S. Brouskari 1974. *The Acropolis Museum.* Athens.

W. Deyhle 1969. "Meisterfragen der archaischen Plastik Attikas." *AM* 84:1–64.

E. D. Francis and M. Vickers 1981. *Proc. Cambr. Philol. Soc.* 207:97sqq.

J. Frel 1982. "Notes on Some Archaic Attic Sculpture." Getty *MJ* 10:95–104.

K. F. Johansen 1951. *The Attic Grave-Reliefs.* Copenhagen.

D. C. Kurtz and J. Boardman 1971. *Greek Burial Customs.* Ithaca, N.Y.

G. Lippold 1950. *Die Griechische Plastik.* Munich.

H. Payne 1954. *Archaic Marble Sculpture from the Acropolis.* New York.

P. Reuterswärd 1960. *Studien zur Polychromie der Plastik. Griechenland und Rom.* Stockholm.

G. Richter 1944. "Polychromy in Greek Sculpture, with Special Reference to the Archaic Gravestones in the Metropolitan Museum." *AJA* 48:321–333.

G. Richter 1961. *The Archaic Gravestones of Attica.* London.

G. Richter 1968. *Korai.* London.

G. Richter 1970. *Kouroi.* London.

B. Schmalz 1983. *Griechische Grabreliefs.* Heidelberg.

E. Touloupa 1983. *Ta enaetia glypta tou naou tou Apollonos Daphniphorou stin Eretria,* Ioannina.

(The two last publications could be considered only in footnote references.)

Index by Museum

Photographs/Credits

Unless stated here, all photographs are provided by the institution that owns the object.

Deutsches Archäologisches Institut, Athens	15a, 15b, 17, 25, 26, 27, 31, 33, 37, 43, 44, 45a, 45b, 46, 47, 48, 51, 52, 53, 56, 59
Deutsches Archäologisches Institut, Rome	3a
F. Mozzana, Rome	8
A. Mulas, Rome	7

Photography of Getty Museum works of art by Donald Hull and Penelope Potter.
Drawings (figs. 2, 23, 24, 38, 64) by Martha Breen Bredemeyer.
Designed by Patrick Dooley.
Production supervised by Karen Schmidt.
Typography by Typographic Service, Inc., Los Angeles, California.
Printing by Gardner/Fulmer Lithograph, Los Angeles, California.